DICTIONARY
of
SPORTS
QUOTATIONS

DICTIONARY
of
SPORTS
QUOTATIONS

Compiled by
BARRY LIDDLE

ROUTLEDGE & KEGAN PAUL
London and New York

First published in 1987 by
Routledge & Kegan Paul Ltd
11 New Fetter Lane, London EC4P 4EE

Published in the USA by
Routledge & Kegan Paul Inc.
in association with Methuen Inc.
29 West 35th Street, New York, NY 10001

Phototypeset in Linotron Caledonia
by Input Typesetting Ltd, London
and printed in Great Britain
by T J Press (Padstow) Ltd
Padstow, Cornwall

© Barry Liddle 1987

Library of Congress Cataloging in Publication Data

Dictionary of sports quotations.
Includes index.
1. Sports—Quotations, maxims, etc.
I. Liddle, Barry.
GV706.8.D53   1987   796'.0321   86–21922

British Library CIP Data also available
ISBN 0–7102–0785–9

CONTENTS

PREFACE

The *Dictionary of Sports Quotations* is not a collection of the mistakes made by sports commentators, nor the ghosted thoughts of sportsmen. Neither is it a complete record of everything worth preserving. No book could ever be that. The object here has been to select quotations for their bearing on the human condition, for their profundity and for the way in which they provide a balanced insight into individual sports and related issues. At least – that has been the intention.

The ideal of a Dictionary embracing all sports had to be tempered against the availability of material and the compiler's access to it. A certain degree of frustration followed from the fact that in several sports the literature is restricted to technical manuals, ghosted autobiographies and/or factual newspaper reports.

As a general observation and despite the contributions of many outstanding writers, it seems to be a truism that sport as a whole fares badly in comparison with other bodies of literature. Perhaps this situation parallels the role of sport as a diversion from, or at best an adjunct to, the more important things in life. This of course is not to denigrate its importance within that position as a metaphysical experience, as a window on the prevailing morality and as a force for good.

No book of quotations can ever be entirely free from errors, and whilst every effort has been made to avoid them here, some will undoubtedly remain. Apologies are therefore offered in equal measure to the reader and to the author of the work quoted.

This is a small book covering a large subject. If the reader has any suggestions for inclusion in a later edition, they would be most welcome if accompanied by the original source and sent c/o 162 Grange Road, Hartlepool, Cleveland TS26 8LX, England.

The research for this book took place in several libraries around the country. In each was a helpful librarian. Thanks are therefore due at the Universities of Exeter, Leicester, London, Loughborough, and Newcastle, to the Polytechnics of Leicester and Teesside, and the Public Libraries in Croydon, Exeter, Hartlepool, Leicester, Middlesbrough and Newcastle. A special thank you is owed to the staff in the main reading room at the British Museum in London.

This book began as an enjoyable if partial therapy for the frustrations of unemployment. At that time and subsequently I was deeply grateful to my brother Brian and his wife Florence and to several friends for their support and encouragement, amongst them Tina Durant, Andy Rees, Philippa James, Pete Hodgkinson, Ann Lahiff, Greg Riddle, Bob Illidge, Steve Carse and Lyn Glew, who also typed the final manuscript. Above all, this book is dedicated to my parents – two fine decent people.

HOW TO USE THE DICTIONARY

THE ARRANGEMENT OF QUOTATIONS

Within each sport/topic the arrangement is alphabetical by author's surname. Under each author, the arrangement is alphabetical by title of the source from which the quotation is taken.

When more than one quotation is taken from a given source, the arrangement is chronological. Books are listed by page; diaries, journals, magazines and newspapers by date and if appropriate by page; and plays by act, scene and first line. 'Ibid.' has been used alongside the numerical source reference on these occasions in place of the full reference. 'Ibid.' on its own refers silently to the last numerical source given.

A quotation by author X found in a work by author Y is included in the alphabetical arrangement under X's name. Author Y's name is then given on a separate line folllowed by the full reference to Y's work and the page on which X's quotation can be found.

All quotations appear in the form in which they are given in the source quoted. There has been no correction of syntax or spelling. An explanatory note does, however, follow some quotations to place them in context.

A date in brackets refers to the first year of publication, all other dates refer to the edition from which the quotation is taken.

References to Shakespeare relate to W. J. Craig (ed.), *The Complete Works of William Shakespeare*, 1980.

TO FIND QUOTATIONS ON A PARTICULAR SPORT OR TOPIC

First use the List of Sports and Topics and then the Subject Index. The latter is alphabetically arranged by key word. Under each key word, the arrangement is alphabetical by sport/topic. Each entry includes part of the quotation to place it in context, the key word is then abbreviated.

The reference relating to each entry consists of a word and a number. The former indicates the sport/topic and the latter the number of the quotation within that sport/topic. The reference is separated from the entry by a comma. For example an entry under 'Sport' reads:

'true s. is amateur, Amateurism 7'

This refers to the 7th quotation under the topic 'Amateurism'.

TO FIND QUOTATIONS BY A PARTICULAR AUTHOR

Consult the Author Index. The arrangement is alphabetical by author's surname. Under each author, the arrangement is alphabetical by sport/topic. As with the Subject Index, the reference for each entry consists of a topic word and a number of the quotation within that topic.

LIST OF SPORTS AND TOPICS

AMATEURISM/
PROFESSIONALISM

1 The athlete who chooses to be paid for sport is no less truly a
sportsman.
Roger Bannister
'The Meaning of Athletic Performance', in E. Jokl and E. Simon
(ed.), *International Research in Sport and Physical Education*,
1964, p. 72.

2 . . . the only true amateurs in sport these days are those who
are no good at it.
Christopher Brasher
Mexico 1968: A Diary of the XIXth Olympiad, 1968, p. 19.

3 Excess begets Nemesis: the Nemesis of excess in athletics is
professionalism, which is the death of all true sport.
E. N. Gardiner
Athletics of the Ancient World, 1930, p. 99.

4 The only real amateur, in my book, is the one who pays his
own expenses.
Vivian Jenkins
Rugby World, vol. 12, no. 3, Mar., 1972, p. 3.

5 Hypocrisy is truly the chief culprit where amateurism is
concerned.
James W. Keating
'The Ethics of Competition and its Relation to some Moral
Problems in Athletics',
in R. G. Osterhoudt (ed.), *The Philosophy of Sport:
A Collection of Original Essays*, 1973, p. 171.

6 Let's be honest. A proper definition of an amateur today is one
who accepts cash, not checks.
Jack Kelly Jr
(U.S.A. Olympic Committee Vice President)
'Scorecard', *Sports Illustrated*, Feb. 8, 1982.

7 The only true sport is amateur.
   René Maheu
   'Cultural Anthropology', in E. Jokl and E. Simon (ed.),
   International Research in Sport and Physical Education, 1964,
   p. 11.

8 The more that the historian looks for the halcyon days of 'pure'
   amateurism, the more they recede from view.
   Tom McNab
   Athletics Weekly, vol. 26, no. 37, Sep. 9, 1972, p. 26.

ANGLING

1 Trout-Fishing of any kind is now difficult to get, and for really
   good fishing, the disciple of Izaac Walton must travel far, and
   fish fine and far off.
   'Avon'
   How I Became a Sportsman, 1888, p. 164.

2 Fishing differs from all other sports in one essential detail; it is
   the only sport, in which the quarry has to co-operate and play
   its own active and willing part.
   Vivian Bailey
   Come Fishing and Shooting, 1961, p. 151.

3 The Black-a-brook might have been absolutely guiltless of trout,
   for all I saw rising there. It was a veritable watery city of the
   dead.
   F. B. Doveton
   A Fisherman's Fancies, 1895, p. 198.

4 We live in an age of applied science, an age in which angling
   has progressed from a bumbling bucolic pastime to a sport of
   considerable discernment.
   David Carl Forbes
   Successful Roach Fishing, p. 14.

5 As between the salmon and the trout I hesitate to express a preference.
Lord Home
Border Reflections, 1979, p. 95.

6 It was not his skill but his approach that made Walton the father of anglers.
T. C. Kingsmill Moore ('Saracen')
A Man May Fish, 1979, preface, p. xi.

7 No one but a master or a fool is dogmatic about fishing, and I have no pretensions to be the one nor wish to appear the other.
T. C. Kingsmill Moore ('Saracen')
Ibid.

8 The sea trout has as many names as royalty.
T. C. Kingsmill Moore ('Saracen')
Ibid., p. 121.

9 No one will ever know all there is to know about angling, but the angler's pleasure will always be in direct proportion to his understanding.
Larry Koller
The Treasury of Angling, 1966, intro.

10 There are not many men who come to fishing late in life – the fascination for the mysterious, half-seen things in the water and the desire to catch them is born in one and it needs little encouragement or opportunity to begin.
John Marchington
Sportsman's Bag, 1975, p. 52.

11 What is emphatic in angling is made so by the long silences – the unproductive periods.
Thomas McGuane
An Outside Chance: Essays on Sport by Thomas McGuane, 1980, p. 3.

12 This day Mr. Caesar told me a pretty experiment of his, of Angling with a Minikin, a gut-string varnished over, which keeps it from swelling and is beyond any hair for strength and smallness – the secret I like mightily.
Samuel Pepys
The Diary of Samuel Pepys, Mar. 18, 1667.

13 All rods can catch fish: their success depends on the hand that
uses them.
Charles Ritz

A Fly Fisher's Life, prepared in collaboration
with John Piper, 1972, p. 57.

14 Fly rods are like women: they won't play if they're maltreated!
Charles Ritz

Ibid.

15 Give me mine angle; we'll to the river: there –
My music playing far off – I will betray
Tawny-finn'd fishes; my bended hook shall
 pierce
Their slimy jaws; and, as I draw them up,
I'll think them every one an Antony,
And say 'Ah, ha!' you're caught.
William Shakespeare

(Cleopatra), *Antony and Cleopatra*, act II, sc. V, l. 10.

16 Twas merry when
You wager'd on your angling; when your diver
Did hang a salt-fish on his hook, which he
With fervency drew up.
William Shakespeare

(Charmian), Ibid., act II, sc. V, l. 16.

17 The pleasant'st angling is to see the fish
Cut with her golden oars the silver stream,
And greedily devour the treacherous bait.
William Shakespeare

(Ursula), *Much Ado about Nothing*, act III, sc. I, l. 26.

18 (*Third Fisherman*) Master, I marvel how the fishes live in the
 sea.
(*First Fisherman*) Why, as men do a-land; the great ones eat up
 the little ones.
William Shakespeare

Pericles, Prince of Tyre, act II, sc. I, l. 29.

19 (*Aside*) How from the finny subject of the sea
These fishers tell the infirmities of men;

And from their watery empire recollect
All that may men approve or men detect!
(*Aloud*) Peace be at your labour, honest fisherman.
William Shakespeare

> (Pericles), Ibid., act II, sc. I, l. 53.

20 (*Second Fisherman*) Canst thou catch any fishes then?
(*Pericles*) I never practised it.
(*Second Fisherman*) Nay then thou wilt starve, sure;
for here's nothing to be got now-a-days unless
thou canst fish for 't.
William Shakespeare

> Ibid., act II, sc. I, l. 71.

21 (*Second Fisherman*) Help, master, help! here's a fish
hangs in the net, like a poor man's right in the
law; 'twill hardly come out.
William Shakespeare

> Ibid., act II, sc. I, l. 126.

22 No one ever did consistently well with unsuitable tackle.
Sidney Spencer

> *Ways of Fishing*, 1972, p. 17.

23 Moonlight may be magic to some people but it holds no magic
for fishers – I think.
Sidney Spencer

> Ibid., p. 44.

24 The vocation of being an angler is filled with unending interest
but it has to be, and often truly is, an attitude of mind and a
consequent way of life.
Sidney Spencer

> Ibid., p. 217.

25 The fish is the hunter, the angler is the hunted.
Richard Waddington

> *Catching Salmon*, 1978, p. 7.

26 And for Winter flie-fishing it is as useful as an Almanack out of
date.
Izaac Walton

> *The Compleat Angler*, 1676, To the Reader.

27 . . . Angling me be said to be so like the Mathematicks, that it can ne'r be fully learnt . . .
Izaac Walton

Ibid.

28 I shall stay him no longer than to wish him a rainy evening to read this following Discourse; and that (if he be an honest Angler) the East wind may never blow when he goes a Fishing.
Izaac Walton

Ibid.

29 . . . Angling is somewhat like Poetry, men are born so: . . .
Izaac Walton

Ibid., part I, ch. 1.

30 (Angling) . . . It is worthy the Knowledge and practice of a wise man.
Izaac Walton

Ibid.

31 . . . Angling will prove to be so pleasant, that it will prove to be like Vertue, a reward to itself.
Izaac Walton

Ibid.

32 I am (Sir) a brother of the Angle . . .
Izaac Walton

Ibid.

33 O Sir, doubt not but that Angling is an Art; . . .
Izaac Walton

Ibid.

34 An excellent Angler and now with God.
Izaac Walton
(Tribute to Sir George Hastings)

Ibid., ch. 4.

35 . . . Fishing is an Art, or at least, it is an Art to catch fish.
Izaac Walton

Ibid., ch. 5.

36 The Carp is the Queen of Rivers: a stately, a good, and a very
   subtil fish . . .
   Izaac Walton

Ibid., ch. 9.

37 I love any Discourse of Rivers, and Fish and fishing . . .
   Izaac Walton

Ibid., ch. 18.

ARCHERY

1 As straight as an arrow.
  Anonymous

2 It is the very difficulty of hitting that round target with its
  bright and open countenance that makes archery so engrossing.
  Alice B. Leigh
  'Ladies Archery', in C. J. Longman and Col. H. Walrond (ed.),
  Archery, 1894, p. 384.

3 One of the great charms of archery is its independence.
  Alice B. Leigh

Ibid., p. 385.

4 Archers with a bad style may make some occasional very good
  scores, or even take a good place for a few seasons, but they
  cannot be depended upon for lasting.
  Alice B. Leigh

Ibid., p. 389.

5 To some of us archery is a matter of life and death; and we
  wear ourselves out, mind and body, in our endeavours to hit
  the centre of the target, but, after all, it is only an amusement,
  and worrying is quite as fatal in this case as it is in others.
  Alice B. Leigh

Ibid., p. 391.

6   For ages the bow was man's most efficient instrument in the chase, and for ages it was his most deadly weapon in war.
    C. J. Longman
    C. J. Longman and Col. H. Walrond (ed.), *Archery*, 1894, p. 1.

7   . . . neither dancing, nor hunting, nor any other sport has played a part in the history of the world which can compare with that of archery.
    C. J. Longman
                                                                    Ibid.

8   (We) walked over the fields of Kingsland and back again, a walk I think I have not taken these twenty years but puts me in mind of my boy's time, when I boarded at Kingsland and used to shoot my bow and arrows in these fields.
    Samuel Pepys
                        The Diary of Samuel Pepys, May 12, 1667.

9   A well-experienc'd archer hits the mark
    His eye doth level at.
    William Shakespeare
                (Antiochus, King of Antioch), *Pericles, Prince of Tyre*,
                                                    act I, sc. I, l. 164.

10 Draw, archers, draw your arrows to the head!
    William Shakespeare
                (King Richard), *The Tragedy of King Richard the Third*,
                                                    act V, sc. III, l. 340.

11 Among the arts that have been carried to a high degree of perfection in this kingdom, there is no one more conspicuous than that of Archery.
    Joseph Strutt
                The Sports and Pastimes of the People of England,
                                                    1830, book II, p. 48.

ATHLETES

1 Being a successful person (or athlete) is not a fortuitous, or lucky happening. It is the end of something often well-planned for, worked for and earned. It can, indeed must, be based on inherited factors.
Percy Wells Cerutty
Success in Sport and Life, 1967, p. 137.

2 From little-league sports up through the professional ranks, the athlete's role is fixated in institutionalized adolescence.
Harry Edwards
Sociology of Sport, 1973, p. 177.

3 The rodeo cowboy represents the last frontier of the pure, unpampered athlete.
Gordon Hansen
Quoted by Robert Creamer.
'Scorecard', *Sports Illustrated*, No. 9, 1970, p. 13.

4 The athlete does not embark upon a sport but upon a way of life.
W. R. Loader
Testament of a Runner, 1960, p. 30.

5 Pressure does crazy things to athletes. Some love it, thrive on it. Others choke on it. Most learn to live with it. A few go nuts!
Herman L. Masin
Scholastic Coach, Nov., 1980, p. 19.

6 The taboos surrounding 'nerve' and 'nerves' in sport are many, for the sportsman is often cast in the role of fear frontiersman.
Angela Potmore
Playing on Their Nerves: The Sport Experiment, 1979, p. 27.

7 Of all the psychological difficulties to beset sportsmen under pressure, indecisiveness seems the most damaging to performance.
Angela Potmore
Ibid., p. 67.

8 Being a role model is as integral a part of the athlete's world as artificial turf and artificial friends.
Peter Richmond

Miami Herald, Nov. 25, 1984.

9 The essential psychological ingredient in any world class athlete is the drive to excel in the toughest possible competition.
The Final Report of the President's Commission on Olympic Sports, vol. 1, Jan., 1977, p. 3.

10 The need to compete with other athletes and with oneself and with Nature is the driving force of all athletes.
Rex Van Rossum

Track Events, 1964, p. 11.

11 An athlete's sporting career is determined by the length of time he can go on striving for better results.
Yuri Vlasov

Sport in the USSR, Jun. 1976, p. 17.

ATHLETICS

1 I leapt at the tape like a man taking his last spring to save himself from the chasm that threatens to engulf him.
Roger Bannister
(On running the first sub-four minute mile, May 6, 1954)
First Four Minutes, 1955, p. 192.

2 I sometimes think that running has given me a glimpse of the greatest freedom a man can ever know, because it results in the simultaneous liberation of both body and mind.
Roger Bannister

Ibid., p. 205.

3 Running races should be absolutely forbidden to men over 27 years of age. Between 30 and 40, a man may indulge in running at a moderate pace for exercise, but not in races. Men over 60

years of age should never run at all for anything, not even to catch a train.
James Cantlie

Physical Efficiency, 1906, p. 179.

4 Running without grace, beauty or elegant style, the marathoner confronts distance, weather, terrain and endless time in an intense struggle to discover how well-tempered is the gentle fiber of his flesh, how stern is the tinsel thread of his will.
Crispin Cusack

'Transcendental Runner', in The Editors of *Runner's World Magazine* (ed.), *The Complete Runner*, 1974, p. 18.

5 Sound field event coaching should have three bones: a wishbone on which to fix goals and ideals; a backbone with which to maintain persistence; and a funny bone with which all the work can be made to seem worth while.
J. Kenneth Doherty

Modern Track and Field (1953), 1964, principle 28, p. 298.

6 The pole vaulter, early in his career, must learn that the mind is something to think with not just for worrying.
Dr R. V. Ganslen

Mechanics of the Pole Vault, 1973, p. 5.

7 If you define poetry as the right words in the right order, then good running is the right movements in the right tempo.
W. R. Loader

Testament of a Runner, 1960, p. 1.

8 The true sprinter is, by nature, necessity and training a physical spendthrift . . .
Brian Mitchell

Athletics Weekly, vol. 26, no. 34, Aug. 19, 1972, p. 32.

9 I never had technique.
Al Oerter
(World record holder and four times Olympic discus champion)
Quoted by Neil Amdur.

The New York Times, May 16, 1978.

10 Mention that you are a hammer thrower to someone who is not an athletics enthusiast and you will be met with any reaction

from a puzzled frown to raucous laughter. If you have the misfortune to say it to a groundsman you may face physical violence.
Howard Payne

Hammer Throwing, 1969, p. 7.

11   . . . I went by water to White-hall to the Privy Seale; and that done, with Mr. Moore and Creed to Hidepark by coach and saw a fine foot-race, three times round the park, between an Irishman and Crow that was once my Lord Claypooles footman.
Samuel Pepys

The Diary of Samuel Pepys, Aug. 10, 1660.

12   My aim has been to win, first against myself and my reluctant body, and secondly against the best athletes, not by stopwatch timing but in races.
Gordon Pirie

Running Wild, 1961, p. 12.

13   In many ways I'm a dedicated fanatic, but I don't let it interfere with my vices!
Arthur Rowe

Champion in Revolt, 1963, p. 28.

14   All the greats in athletics have been supreme individualists.
Arthur Rowe

Ibid., p. 75.

15   The Loneliness of the Long Distance Runner.
Alan Sillitoe

Book title.

16   I once threw the javelin rather promisingly until my arm glassed up.
John Steinbeck

Sports Illustrated, Dec. 20, 1965.

17   Runners are second only to gamblers in their search for a new system, something that will turn them from scrubbers to supermen, if not overnight, at least by next Saturday.
Bruce Tulloh

Foreword in Anton Ward, *Modern Distance Running*, 1964.

18 The elevation of athletics is a recognition that it is the sport of supreme endeavour; the sport where man pits himself not only against other men, but also against the limitations which Nature has imposed upon him; the sport where frontiers of human endurance are attained and surpassed.
Rex Van Rossum

Track Events, 1964, p. 11.

19 Athletics is not a sport for the half-hearted. It is an all-or-nothing sport. There is nothing to be won, no honour, glory, pleasure or satisfaction from dabbling in it.
Rex Van Rossum

Ibid., p. 12.

20 An athlete cannot run with money in his pockets. He must run with hope in his heart and dreams in his head.
Emil Zatopek
Quoted by Christopher Brasher.

The Observer, Sep. 12, 1982.

BADMINTON

1 The beginning of badminton is the co-ordination of hand and eye.
Fred Brundle

Teach Yourself Badminton, 1964, p. 15.

2 The shuttle is a prima donna . . .
Pat Davis

The Guinness Book of Badminton, 1983, p. 32.

3 The more you play, the faster you become; the faster you become, the earlier you take the shuttle; the earlier you take the shuttle, the more alternatives are open to you, the more winners are on.
David Hunt
Quoted by Pat Davis.

Ibid., p. 69.

4   (Badminton) A poetic pastime for the Parish Hall.
John Oliff

Ibid., p. 41.

5   To deceive to deceive to deceive is the art of badminton.
Sir George Thomas

Ibid.

BALLOONING/ FLYING/GLIDING

1   Flying is not handed out on a plate, it has to be paid for!
Anonymous

2   The ability to stay aloft and even gain altitude without an engine makes soaring a most fascinating combination of nature, science, and skill.
William T. Carter
    Soaring: The Sport of Flying Sailplanes, 1974, ch. 1, p. 1.

3   A pilot may treat soaring as a hobby, a sport, a technical skill, a competitive game, a personal challenge, or as a satisfying pastime.
William T. Carter

Ibid., p. 4.

4   Gliding is largely a matter of ups and downs – a battle against gravity.
Peter Scott

5   Gliding is a team sport, up to the point at which you become airborne.
Bill Scull

Gliding and Soaring, 1977, p. 9.

6 Ballooning is an art, not a science, and is surely the only form of flying, or even locomotion where one has no controls to turn left or right, accelerate or brake.
Christine Turnbull
Hot Air Ballooning, 1970, p. 8.

BASEBALL

1 Whoever wants to know the heart and mind of America had better learn baseball.
Jacques Barzun
Quoted by Michael Novak.
The Joys of Sports, 1976, part 1.

2 Hitting a baseball could well be the single most difficult skill in sport.
Jim Bowen
Scholastic Coach, Mar., 1980, p. 22.

3 I think it's all right; it keeps the parents off the streets.
Rocky Bridges
(On Little League Baseball)
'Scorecard', *Sports Illustrated*, Mar. 2, 1964, p. 8.

4 I thought baseball was a sport when I became a commissioner. I was mistaken. The semibandits own it.
Happy Chandler
'Scorecard', *Sports Illustrated*, Nov. 19, 1962.

5 In its urban setting baseball tended to stress its rural origins and attachments. In doing so, baseball tied itself to one of the most historically enduring and powerful myths in American culture.
Richard C. Crepeau
(On Baseball in 1920/30)
'Urban and Rural Images in Baseball',
Journal of Popular Culture, vol. IX, no. 2, Fall, 1975, p. 315.

6 No matter how limited a baseball player may be, he should be able to do at least two things well – run the bases and bunt.
Rod Delmonico
Scholastic Coach, Mar., 1983.

7 Once an asylum for amiable eccentrics, it has become a lifeless charade by actors who look as impersonal as motorcycle cops.
Stanley Frank
(On Baseball)
Sports Illustrated, Aug. 27, 1962, p. 18.

8 Baseball lives at the centre of a never-flagging whirl of irreconcilable opinions.
Paul Gardner
Nice Guys Finish Last: Sport and American Life, 1975, p. 65.

9 A great catch is like watching girls go by – the last one you see is always the prettiest.
Bob Gibson
'Scorecard', *Sports Illustrated*, Jun. 1, 1964, p. 19.

10 I take a national view of the American League and an American view of the National League.
Vice President Hubert Humphrey
(When asked which league would win the World Series 1967)
'Scorecard', *Sports Illustrated*, Sep. 11, 1967, p. 19.

11 In all but a very few instances baseball fails to generate any kind of dramatic unity.
E. F. Kaelin
'The Well-Played Game: Notes Toward an Aesthetics of Sport',
in Ellen W. Gerber (ed.), *Sport and the Body:
A Philosophical Symposium*, 1974, p. 307.

12 Nobody gets a kick out of baseball anymore, because big salaries and the pension fund have made it a more serious business than running a bank.
Rabbit Maranville
Quoted by Stanley Frank.
Sports Illustrated, Aug. 27, 1962, p. 18.

13 Baseball is a Lockean game, a kind of contract theory in ritual form, a set of atomic individuals who assent to patterns of limited co-operation in their mutual interest.
Michael Novak
The Joys of Sports, 1976, part 1, p. 59.

14 The origins of modern baseball are shrouded in history, but it is a well-established fact that baseball was the first professional sport to appeal to the masses.
George H. Sage
Sport and American Society: Selected Readings, 1970, p. 156.

15 Every pitcher is a creature of habit.
Henry A. Thomas
Scholastic Coach, Mar., 1980, p. 26.

16 All fielders must have good instincts.
Henry A. Thomas
Scholastic Coach, Dec., 1983.

17 Though it is a team game by definition, it is actually a series of loosely connected individual efforts.
Bill Veeck
Scholastic Coach, Dec., 1983.

18 Baseball is an island of surety in a changing world.
Bill Veeck
Quoted by Jonathon Green.
A Dictionary of Contemporary Quotations, 1982, p. 345.

19 Catchers have to do two things supremely well – handle pitchers and discourage stealers.
Jerry Weinstein
Scholastic Coach, Mar., 1981, p. 28.

20 Baseball gives every American boy a chance to excel, not just to be as good as someone else but to be better than someone else. This is the nature of man and the name of the game . . .
Ted Williams
'Scorecard', *Sports Illustrated*, Aug. 8, 1966.

BASKETBALL

1   I'd rather play a pinball machine than watch a basketball game today. You can score the same number of points.
Chick Davies
'Scorecard', *Sports Illustrated*, Mar. 23, 1964, p. 12.

2   Basketball . . . is staying in after school in your underwear.
(Gabriel), in *Drive He Said* (Col. 1970).
Quoted by Ronald Bergan.
Sports in the Movies, 1982, p. 144.

3   It is an axiom that good players without a good coach make a mediocre team.
Alexander Gomelsky
Sport in the USSR, Dec., 1981, p. 14.

4   Quick guys get tired. Big guys don't shrink.
Marv Harshman
(On selecting Basketball players)
'Scorecard', *Sports Illustrated*, Jan. 30, 1984.

5   The good coach is much more than a basketball instructor for consciously or subconsciously he assumes the role of an educationalist carrying his influence far beyond basketball itself.
B. Jagger
Basketball: Coaching and Playing, p. 11.

6   Basketball has so much showboating you'd think it was invented by Jerome Kern.
Art Spender
'Coaches Corner', *Scholastic Coach*, Dec., 1983, p. 60.

7   To achieve a minimally acceptable level of success, a college coach must be either a very good coach or a very good recruiter. To experience great success, he must be both a good coach and a good recruiter.
Dr W. F. Stier Jr
Scholastic Coach, May/Jun., 1983.

8 Three things are vital to success in basketball – condition, fundamentals, and working together as a team. I said that when I played, I said that when I first started coaching, I said that last year, and I will keep on saying it next year, the year after, and for the rest of my life.
John Wooden
They Call Me Coach, 1972, p. 123.

BILLIARDS/ SNOOKER/POOL

1 The Billiard table is the paradise of the ball.
A. E. Crawley
The Book of the Ball, 1913, p. 201.

2 Dressing a pool player in a tuxedo is like putting whipped cream on a hot dog.
Minnesota Fats
'Scorecard', *Sports Illustrated*, Apr. 4, 1966, p. 24.

3 . . . a billiard player of average ability can always turn his hand to playing quite a good game of snooker, whereas a fair snooker player rarely can turn his hand to playing a good game of billiards.
Jack Karnehm
Billiards and Snooker, 1973, p. 117.

4 If snooker hadn't existed TV would surely have had to invent it.
Geoffrey Nicholson
The Observer, Apr. 22, 1984.

5 Up, all of us, and to Billiards –
Samuel Pepys
The Diary of Samuel Pepys, Jul. 17, 1665.

6   After dinner to Billiards, where I won an angel.
Samuel Pepys

Ibid., Sep. 11, 1665.

7   No one ever became so good at a ball game that they could play it like a machine.
John Pulman

Tackle Snooker, 1974, p. 142.

8   Let it alone, let's to billiards.
William Shakespeare

(Cleopatra, Queen of Egypt),
Antony and Cleopatra, act II, sc. IV, l. 3.

9   Indians are perhaps the only people who still place the austere skills of billiards above the gaudy promiscuity of snooker.
Eric Silver

The Guardian, Aug. 8, 1985, p. 1.

BODYBUILDING

1   . . . it is difficult to respect a sport that has 'posing' as part of its jargon.
Jasmine Birtles

The Guardian, 1975.

2   Body-builders do not throw their weight around – they flaunt it.
David Hunn

The Observer, Jul. 28, 1985, p. 43.

3   Posing is a performing art.
Arnold Schwarzenegger
Quoted by Jasmine Birtles.

The Guardian, 1975.

BOWLS

1 There is plenty of time to win this game and to thrash the
  Spaniards too.
  Sir Francis Drake (Attributed)
  Quoted by A. and V. Palmer.
  *Quotations in History: A Dictionary of Historical Quotations
  c 800 A.D. to the Present*, 1976, p. 70.

2 Bowls is a game which can be played without the least loss of
  dignity; and as a pastime it appeals more perhaps to the sober
  and sedate than to the superabundant energies of youth.
  F. W. Hackwood
  Old English Sports, 1907, p. 175.

3 Although there are a few diehards who would like to think
  differently, Bowls has never been a prerogative of the male sex.
  Alfred H. Haynes
  The Story of Bowls, 1972, p. 93.

4 In general bowlers are a hardy race.
  Alfred H. Haynes
  Ibid., p. 130.

5 Stiffness is an occupational hazard so far as bowlers are
  concerned.
  C. M. Jones
  Bowls: How to Become a Champion, 1972, p. 64.

6 However profoundly one studies and understands the theories
  of bowls techniques, tactics and temperament, the ultimate test
  comes always in competition on the green.
  C. M. Jones
  Ibid., p. 145.

7 Was there ever man had such luck! When I kissed the jack,
  upon an up-cast to be hit away! I had a hundred pound on't;
  William Shakespeare
  (Cloten), *Cymbeline*, act II, sc. I, l. 1.

8 What I have lost to-day at bowls I'll win to-night of him.
   William Shakespeare
   (Cloten), *Cymbeline*, act II, sc. I, l. 55.

9 (*Queen*) What sport shall we devise here in this garden,
   To drive away the heavy thought of care?
   (*First Lady*) Madam, we'll play at bowls.
   William Shakespeare
   The Tragedy of King Richard the Second, act III, sc. IV, l. 1.

BOXING

1 I am the Greatest!
   Muhammad Ali

2 The fast money attracts the boxers and the schemers. But the boxers bleed, the schemers smirk. The boxers depart, the schemers survive. It has always been that way in boxing, and it always will be.
   Dave Anderson
   The New York Times, Apr. 24, 1977.

3 He was so strong that he could write his name with an eighty-four pound weight dangling from his little finger; and there must have been many boxers of his day who could not have written theirs for an eighty-four pound prize.
   Denzil Batchelor
   (On Gentleman John Jackson)
   Big Fight: The Story of World Championship Boxing, 1954, p. 31.

4 By and large, it may be said that the best training for a career in the ring is fighting: not boxing, but fighting.
   Denzil Batchelor
   Ibid., p. 228.

5 The boxer, if he would be a champion, must strive to destroy his opponent – not, of course, to kill him (for that would be a waste of energy), but to wipe him out of the world for ten seconds on end.
Denzil Batchelor

Ibid.

6 Boxers are as various as finger-prints: no two are alike.
Denzil Batchelor
Gods With Gloves On, 1947, p. 4.

7 There have been champions who hated the game and animated punch-bags who couldn't have enough of it.
Denzil Batchelor

Ibid.

8 The boxer is a round peg in a square ring, manipulated by others for profit.
Ronald Bergan
Sports in the Movies, 1982, p. 14.

9 Boxing is a subject which seems to give rise to approval, interest, indifference, disgust and violent argument.
Dr J. L. Blonstein
Boxing Doctor, 1965, p. 11.

10 The glove is there to guard the hand from damage, not add to its power. Therein lies the demarcation line between boxing today and boxing yesterday.
Harry Carpenter
Boxing an Illustrated History, 1982.

11 Behind the scenes, professional boxing has always been seedy, and endlessly fascinating.
Harry Carpenter
The Hardest Game, 1981, p. 47.

12 The psychology of boxing seems to be but little understood by the average boxer, and yet this often is the pivot upon which contests revolve.
Georges Carpentier
My Methods or Boxing As A Fine Art,
translated by F. Hurdman-Lucas, 1914, p. 19.

13   There exists a tendency to treat boxing as a mere sport demanding little else but an orthodox knowledge of punching, coupled with brute strength. A greater mistake was never made.
Georges Carpentier

Ibid.

14   The conscientious boxer I say, is at once well behaved, a good fellow, a gentleman in nature, and a credit to his country.
Georges Carpentier

Ibid., p. 20.

15   The art of boxing is not acquired, but a gift.
Georges Carpentier

Ibid., p. 26.

16   Boxing is not only a matter for fist to fist or blow for blow, but of clever tactics.
Georges Carpentier

Ibid., p. 37.

17   It is an essential to the modern boxer as water is to life.
Georges Carpentier
(On In-Fighting)

Ibid.

18   . . . there are more ways of stopping punches than there are of delivering them.
Georges Carpentier

Ibid., p. 41.

19   A boxer feeling the pangs of fatigue should, when suffering, always remember that his opponent is in a similar state, more or less – perhaps more.
Georges Carpentier

The Art of Boxing, 1926, p. 34.

20   Attack is only one half of the art of boxing.
Georges Carpentier

Ibid., p. 106.

21   Boxers need somewhere to fight, and that is why we have this square we call a ring.
Henry Cooper
> *Henry Cooper's Book of Boxing*, 1982, round 9, p. 123.

22   Boxing is a game for men, and only for men.
Eugene Corri
> *Thirty Years a Boxing Referee*, 1915, p. 4.

23   If professional boxing is morally indefensible, so are zoos and circuses and those television games that play strip-tease with human dignity.
Guy Deghy
> *Noble and Manly: The History of the National Sporting Club, incorporating The Posthumous Papers of The Pelican Club*, 1956, p. II.

24   Two million dollars gate at one fight! That's some cabbage in any man's language.
Wilfrid Diamond
> (Gate money paid for the Jack Dempsey v. Gene Tunney fight, Sep. 23, 1926) *Blood, Sweat, and Jack Dempsey*, 1953, p. 7.

25   He was always a clean fighter in a dirty game.
Wilfrid Diamond
(On Joe Louis)
> *How Great Was Joe Louis?*, 1955.

26   The heavyweight championship of the world never dropped into anybody's lap. It's on top of a hill, and a mighty steep, slippery hill.
Wilfrid Diamond
> *This Guy Marciano*, 1955, p. 9.

27   Two things about Marciano's career to date stand out like a couple of black eyes at a church supper – he has a punch and he has a manager. Mighty potent is the punch and mighty shrewd was the management.
Wilfrid Diamond
> Ibid., p. 11.

28   Age is a mighty important subject for a champion, because it is the one opponent he can't lick.
Wilfrid Diamond

Ibid., p. 20.

29   Rocky Marciano doesn't need a shillelagh – he had one built into each hand.
Wilfrid Diamond

Ibid., p. 23.

30   The fight racket may be good for those at the top, but for the rank and file it is a heart-breaking as well as a body-breaking business.
Wilfrid Diamond

Ibid., p. 87.

31   There are perhaps few blows more unpleasantly startling than a good left-hand counter which meets you full-face. It opens a spacious firmament to the bewildered eyes, wherein you discover more new planets in a second than the most distinguished astronomer ever observed in a life-time.
Ned (Edward) Donnelly

Self-Defence; or the Art of Boxing, 1879, p. 77.

32   Fighting remember, comes naturally, but not so boxing.
Dai Dower

'The Straight Left', in Frank Butler (ed.),
Success at Boxing, 1956, p. 22.

33   There is one precept a boxer should never forget, and that is that he should never waste a moment between gong and gong.
Jim Driscoll

Ringcraft, 1910, p. 34.

34   A boxer should always cultivate speed above every other quality, save and except stamina, which should, of course, be developed in equal proportion.
Jim Driscoll

Ibid., p. 47.

35   . . . a scrupulously fair boxer is usually badly handicapped in a clinch.
Jim Driscoll

Ibid., p. 64.

36 Boxing conjures up the image of sleazy characters hanging
    around smelly gymnasiums, eagerly seeking fights to fix and
    boxers to buy.
    Anthony O. Edmonds
    'The Second Louis – Schmeling Fight – Sport, Symbol and
    Culture', *Journal of Popular Culture*, vol. VII, no. 1, Summer
                                                    1970, p. 42.

37 If the fight saw the symbolic defeat of German racism, it also,
    according to many observers, witnessed the triumph of Amer-
    ican values.
    Anthony O. Edmonds
                                                    Ibid., p. 46.

38 The constituents of the complete boxer are strength, art,
    courage, activity, the power of bearing blows, a quick eye, and
    wind.
    Thomas Fewtrell
    From *Boxing Reviewed; or the Science of Manual Defence;
    Displayed on Rational Principles. Comprehending A Complete
    Description of the Principal Pugilists From the Earliest Period
    of Broughton's Time to the Present Day*, 1790.
    Quoted by Bohun Lynch.
                                        The Prize Ring, 1925, p. 16.

39 Like a game of chess, boxing, when properly followed, is a
    sport of wits.
    Nat Fleischer
                                        How to Box, 1958, p. 5.

40 You don't need to be a ruffian or a loafer to be a boxer, and
    boxing doesn't lower a young man nor makes a loafer out of
    him. It makes him better.
    Nat Fleischer
                                                    Ibid., p. 7.

41 The judge and the referee must be guided by what they see,
    and not by what others would have them see.
    Nat Fleischer
            How to Judge and How to Referee a Fight, 1962, p. 1.

42 Three of the blackest evils in boxing, other than the control of
    boxers by unsavory characters, are fouls, mismatches and
    odorous decisions.
    Nat Fleischer

    Ibid., p. 5.

43 Some pugilists have an exalted opinion of their fighting ability,
    and therefore labor under the false impression that they cannot
    or are not defeated unless they are knocked out.
    Nat Fleischer

    Ibid., p. 25.

44 If I were a dictator, I would abolish prize fighting in my country
    by decree. I would scrap all rings, burn all boxing gloves and
    never let a youth be taught to strike another with his fist. For
    prize fighting and boxing are stupid, senseless, unappetising,
    inefficient and one hundred per cent useless.
    Paul Gallico
    Quoted by Dr Edith Summerskill.

    The Ignoble Art, 1956, p. 86.

45 I have covered boxing, promoted boxing, watched it, thought
    about it, and after long reflection I cannot find a single thing
    that is good about it either from the point of view of participant
    or spectator.
    Paul Gallico

    Ibid.

46 Wherever men fight, and wherever men talk of boxing, the
    pallid little Welsh collier, Jimmy Wilde, is established as a
    legend – beyond the mists of memory, beyond the rust of time.
    Reg Gutteridge

    Boxing The Great Ones, 1975, p. 142.

47 One of the big secrets of success at boxing, or any sport for
    that matter, is mastering the art of relaxation.
    Len Harvey

    'Tactics', in Frank Butler (ed.), *Success at Boxing*,
    1956, p. 88.

48 . . . boxing being a sport which draws a lot of money, corre-
    spondingly draws a great crowd of spivs, drones and 'wise men'.
    Eugene Henderson

    'Boxing' Teaches a Boy, 1952, p. 3.

49 . . . boxing as a science stands on the most elementary basis –
the stance.
Eugene Henderson

Ibid., p. 6.

50 There are only three means of defence. One, by attack, and
two and three, by blocking and weaving.
Eugene Henderson

Ibid., p. 24.

51 . . . woe betide the boxer who does not use his brains for
defensive work, but uses his skull instead.
Eugene Henderson

Ibid., p. 27.

52 I should be sorry to see Prize-fighting go out. Every art should
be preserved, and the art of defence is surely important . . .
prize-fighting makes people accustomed not to be alarmed at
seeing their own blood or feeling a little pain from a wound.
Doctor Samuel Johnson
Quoted by Fred W. J. Henning.

Some Recollections of the Prize Ring, 1888, ch. 39.

53 I have always considered that boxing really combines all the
finest and highest inclinations of a man – activity, endurance,
science, temper, and, last, but not least, presence of mind.
Lord Lonsdale
Foreword in Eugene Corri, *Thirty Years a Boxing Referee*,
1915.

54 The Noble Art of Boxing is of the extremest antiquity.
Bohun Lynch

The Prize Ring, 1925, p. 1.

55 Maybe all illness results from a failure of communication
between mind and body. It is certainly true of such quick
disease as a knockout.
Norman Mailer

The Fight, 1976, p. 10.

56 For Ali to compose a few words of real poetry would be equal
to an intellectual throwing a good punch.
Norman Mailer

Ibid., p. 18.

57 Boxing is the exclusion of outside influence. A classic discipline.
    Norman Mailer

    Ibid., p. 31.

58 No physical activity is so vain as boxing. A man gets into the
    ring to attract admiration. In no sport, therefore, can you be
    more humiliated.
    Norman Mailer

    Ibid., p. 47.

59 There is agony to elucidate even a small sense of the aesthetic
    out of boxing.
    Norman Mailer

    Ibid., p. 171.

60 Professional boxing is unique among the sports. It is admittedly
    the only sport whose primary objective toward victory is to
    batter and damage an opponent into helplessness and the inca-
    pacity to continue.
    R. A. McCormick
       'Is Professional Boxing Immoral?' in Ellen W. Gerber (ed.),
    Sport and the Body: A Philosophical Symposium, 1974, p. 271.

61 Any supporter of boxing who does not admit to some residual
    ambivalence about its values, who has not wondered in its
    crueller moments if it is worth the candle, must be suspect.
    Hugh McIlvanney
          McIlvanney on Boxing: An Anthology, 1982, p. 13.

62 . . . boxing has always been a primitive trial of the whole man,
    never a mere contest of skill.
    Hugh McIlvanney

    Ibid., p. 84.

63 Fighting is a dirty business as a whole, but the coloured boy
    from 'Bama has done a lot to lift it from the gutter.
    Henry McLemore
    (On Joe Louis)
    Quoted by Margery Miller.
       Brown Bomber: The Life Story of Joe Louis, 1946, p. 108.

64 . . . there is no business like the fight business.
    Freddie Mills
                Twenty Years An Autobiography, 1950, p. 205.

65   Boxing is syllables. You learn them one by one.
Archie Moore
Quoted by Norman Mailer.

The Fight, 1976, p. 188.

66   Boxers are born, not made.
Gilbert Odd

Boxing: The Inside Story, 1978, p. 22.

67   Strength, most undoubtedly, is what the Boxer ought to set out
with, but without art he will succeed but poorly.
One of the Fancy (Later edition found under Pierce Egan the
Elder)
*Boxiana; or Sketches of Ancient and Modern Pugilism; From the
Days of the Renowned Broughton and Slack, To The Heroes of
the Present Milling Era*, 1812, p. 37.

68   The blows given between the eye-brows contribute greatly to
the victory: . . .
One of the Fancy

Ibid., p. 41.

69   Strength and art have been mentioned as the two principal
requisites for a Boxer to possess; but there is another equally
as necessary, and without which no Pugilist can be termed
complete – denominated bottom. In establishing bottom, there
are two things required – wind and spirit, or heart, or wherever
you fix the residence of courage.
One of the Fancy

Ibid., p. 43.

70   Readiness to fight doubles the strength.
John Boyle O'Reilly
Ethics of Boxing and Manly Sport, 1888, p. 74.

71   Boxing leaves out nothing; it exercises the whole man at once
and equally – the trunk, the limbs, the eyes – and the mind.
John Boyle O'Reilly

Ibid., p. 82.

72 (Boxing) It asks more steadiness, self-control, ay, and manly courage, than any other exercise. You must take as well as give – eye to eye, toe to toe, and arm to arm.
Sir Robert Peel
Quoted by John Boyle O'Reilly.

Ibid., p. 1.

73 The reason I am a fight fan to-day – the reason my grandfather was, the reason Old 'Q' was – is that I like action.
The Tenth Marquess of Queensberry

The Sporting Queensberrys, 1942.

74 The glove which I have given him for a favour,
May haply purchase him a box o' the ear;
William Shakespeare

(King Henry), *The Life of King Henry the Fifth*,
act IV, sc. VII, l. 181.

75 Give him a box o' the ear, and that will make 'em red again.
William Shakespeare

(Cade), *The Second Part of King Henry the Sixth*,
act IV, sc. VII, l. 91.

76 Professional boxing is the only sport in which a participant seeks to knock his opponent out in the shortest possible space of time. It is the only sport in which to confess injury and retire is to risk a hostile demonstration from the spectators.
It is the only sport in which wounds inflicted and blood drawn gives colour, zest and a sadistic thrill to the whole performance.
Dr Edith Summerskill

The Ignoble Art, 1956, p. 22.

77 How firm a grip the Prize Ring must have had upon the national taste is evidenced by the phrases which it has left embedded in the language. To 'throw up the sponge', to 'come up smiling', to 'come to the scratch', to 'hit out straight from the shoulder', . . . 'ugly customer' . . .
Thormanby (Pseud. for W. Willmot Dixon)
Boxers and Their Battles, Anecdotal Sketches and Personal
Recollections of Famous Pugilists, 1900, p. 3.

78 Boxing can be a cruel business and I know of no contrast so savage as that between the winner's and the loser's dressing room.
Peter Wilson

> *Boxing's Greatest Prize*, 1982, p. 76.

BULLFIGHTING

1 The bull fight is a pure art.
Ernest Hass
Quoted by C. L. R. James.
> 'The Relationship Between Popular Sport and Fine Art',
> in H. T. A. Whiting and D. W. Masterson (ed.),
> *Readings in the Aesthetics of Sport*, 1974, p. 103.

2 Bullfighting is worthless without rivalry. But with two great bullfighters it becomes a deadly rivalry.
Ernest Hemingway
(Extract from *The Dangerous Summer*)
> *Observer Magazine*, Jun. 16, 1985.

3 Bullfighting is not a cruel sport, but a cruel method of achieving plastic beauty.
John Marks
Quoted by Jonathon Green.
> *Dictionary of Contemporary Quotations*, 1982, p. 343.

CAMPING

1 Tents have been compared to yellow camera-filters: they bring out rain clouds.
Nigel Hunt
> *Illustrated Teach Yourself Camping*, 1969, intro.

2   Camping is not new – any tramp will tell you that.
Nigel Hunt

Ibid., p. 8.

3   Camping of course covers a very wide canvas.
Mark Newton

The Book of Camping, 1970, p. 11.

CANOEING

1   Made of everything from ABS to aluminium to Kevlar to cedar strip, the Canadian canoe is about as ubiquitous in Canada as a McDonalds hamburger wrapper . . .
Nick Adams

Canoeing, no. 60, Dec., 1982, p. 10.

2   L.D. racing needs fitness, first and foremost.
Nigel Hunt

Adventures in Canoeing, 1964, p. 103.

3   On an L.D. race you are more than the man in the cockpit . . . you work in the pits as well.
Nigel Hunt

Ibid.

4   Canoe slaloms are without doubt the most exciting and most spectacular of all branches of canoeing and have a direct appeal to all canoeists and a spectacular interest for everyone.
B. E. Jagger

Canoeing, 1961, p. 109.

5   Slalom is a gruelling sport; it's not just a simple test of speed or skill, it is a combination of speed, precision and stamina . . .
Jennifer Munro

Canoeing, no. 68, Aug., 1983, p. 19.

6   Boats are for work; canoes are for pleasure.
John Boyle O'Reilly

Ethics of Boxing and Manly Sport, 1888, p. 244.

7 Slalom racing is a bit like chess, the straightest path is by no
   means always the quickest.
   Ivars Simanis
                          Sport in the USSR, Nov., 1979, p. 34.

8 I think sporting dignity and victory are concepts that rank on
   the same level.
   Tamas Wichmann
                          Sport in the USSR, Aug., 1980.

CAVING/ POTHOLING

1 Caving is the most absolute of sports.
   C. H. D. Cullingford
      British Caving: An introduction to Speleology, 1962, p. 1.

2 Caving is a physical adventure which leads to adventures of the
   mind.
   Cecil Cullingford
                                        Caving, 1976, p. 5.

3 The physical adventure of caving produces in most cavers a
   thirst for scientific knowledge, so that willy-nilly they become
   speleologists.
   Cecil Cullingford
                                        Ibid., p. 23.

4 The visual beauty of caves is largely one of contrast.
   David Heap
         Potholing: Beneath the Northern Pennines, 1964, p. 4.

5 Caving is like good poetry, for it draws on all the senses as
   much as on the emotions.
   David Heap
                                        Ibid., p. 6.

6   Potholing is a team sport, and as such it involves inter-reliance
as much as self-reliance.
David Heap

Ibid., p. 11.

CLIMBING/ MOUNTAINEERING

1   If anyone should ask me to sum up mountaineering in a few
words I could only string together those words which first come
to mind; struggle, adventure, romance, escapism, sport . . .
Walter Bonatti

On the Heights, translated by Lovett F. Edwards, 1979,
preface.

2   Fear is something that all climbers feel at some time. Without
it there would be no caution.
Joe Brown

The Hard Years: An Autobiography, 1974, p. 17.

3   Between the extremes of aesthetic satisfaction and the spice of
danger – the latter often seen by the layman as the main reason
for mountaineering – the sport has also provided an arena for
the testing of personal performance.
Ronald W. Clarke

Men, Myths and Mountains, 1976, intro.

4   Mountaineering tends to be the sport of the visiting lowlander,
highlanders must be more pragmatic.
John Cleare

Mountaineering, 1980, p. 7.

5   A dangerous mountaineer is a bad mountaineer.
John Cleare

Ibid., p. 8.

6 Certainly mountaineering is an anarchistic sport. Unlike most other sports it does not depend on organisations and officials, competition and referees. It has no rules and its methods and outcome are of importance only to the participants themselves.
John Cleare

Ibid.

7 Rock-climbing is the art of climbing steep rock. At its most aesthetic it has been likened to ballet in a vertical idiom.
John Cleare

Ibid., p. 121.

8 From an eccentric diversion, mountaineering has become a recognizable sport.
John Cleare

Mountains, 1975, p. 17.

9 The blind suppression of justified fear makes heroes, but vastly reduces a climber's life expectancy.
John Cleare

Ibid., p. 65.

10 We climb because it is compulsive and we enjoy it. Why probe for a deeper meaning?
John Cleare

Ibid.

11 Climbs are as old as the hills, but climbs wilfully or gratuitously undertaken belong only to recent times.
Claire Eliane Engel
Mountaineering in the Alps: An Historical Survey, 1971,
p. 17.

12 Every sport, including mountaineering, gets the literature and the adepts it deserves.
Claire Eliane Engel

Ibid., p. 178.

13 Mountains do not change, but the spirit in which they are faced often does.
Claire Eliane Engel

Ibid., p. 207.

14 Climbs are a question not only of skill and strength, but also of moral and intellectual balance.
    Claire Eliane Engel

Ibid., p. 291.

15 One may say that mountains hold up a mirror to the man who wishes to climb them.
    Claire Eliane Engel

Ibid.

16 Mountaineering is a game second only to the greatest and best of man's games – life.
    George Ingle Finch
                    The Making of A Mountain, 1927, p. 11.

17 The mountains are no more homicidal than any other part of nature.
    Charles Gos
        Alpine Tragedy, translated by Malcolm Barnes, 1948, p. 3.

18 Climbing is all about facing problems; the better the problems, the more memorable the climb.
    Anthony Greenbank
                    Climbing for Young People, 1977, p. 6.

19 In speaking of the peculiar merits of mountaineering, a man knows hardly where to begin, much less where to stop.
    Frederic Harrison
                    'Mountaineering', in R. L. G. Irving (ed.),
                            The Mountain Way:
                An Anthology in Prose and Verse, 1938, p. 50.

20 I discovered that even the mediocre can have adventures and even the fearful can achieve.
    Edmund Hillary
                Nothing Venture, Nothing Win, 1975, Foreword.

21 Finally I cut around the back of an extra large hump and then on a tight rope from Tenzing I climbed up a gentle snow ridge to its top. Immediately it was obvious that we had reached our objective. It was 11.30 a.m. and we were on top of Everest!
    Edmund Hillary

Ibid., p. 160.

22 In mountaineering perhaps more than most other activities, it is a golden rule to press on and on no account be dismayed by unfavourable impressions – to rub your nose, as it were, against the obstacle.
Sir John Hunt
The Ascent of Everest, 1953, p. 4.

23 We climb mountains because we like it.
Sir John Hunt
Ibid., p. 8.

24 There are three factors of awe-inspiring magnitude facing those who seek adventure among the highest peaks . . . vertical scale, the climatic conditions and the climbing difficulties.
Sir John Hunt
Ibid., p. 9.

25 Every man must seek the pleasures of mountaineering in his own way.
R. L. G. Irving
'Five Years with Recruits', in Walter Unsworth (ed.), *Selections from the Alpine Journal, Peaks, Passes and Glaciers*, 1981, p. 163.

26 Mountaineering is an elaboration of the simple experience of walking up or down hill.
Francis Keenlyside
Peaks and Pioneers: The Story of Mountaineering, 1975, p. 9.

27 He can call himself a mountaineer when he can deal with mountains.
Walter Larden
Recollections of An Old Mountaineer, 1910, p. 2.

28 Because it is there.
George Leigh Mallory
(In answer to the question; why do you want to climb Mount Everest, Mr. Mallory? – woman reporter)
Quoted by Walter Unsworth
Because it is There, 1973, p. 117.

29 Have we vanquished an enemy? None but ourselves. Have we
    gained success? That word means nothing here. Have we won
    a Kingdom? No . . . and yes. We have achieved an ultimate
    satisfaction . . . fulfilled a destiny . . . To struggle and to under-
    stand – never this last without the other; such is the law . . .
    George Leigh Mallory
                'Pages from a Journal', in Walter Unsworth (ed.),
        Selections from the Alpine Journal, Peaks, Passes and Glaciers,
                                                            1981, p. 181.

30 Even the most spirited mountaineer is not spirit only; he has
    a body attached as well, and an instinct to preserve it . . .
    W. H. Murray
    Foreword in J. E. B. Wright, *The Technique of Mountain-
                                                    eering*, 1955.

31 One of the great joys of mountaineering is that there are no
    imposed rules. In that respect the sport is of all sports thrice
    royal, and the mountaineer his own absolute monarch.
    W. H. Murray
                                                            Ibid.

32 Guides are no foolhardy adventurers: they live, they do their
    job.
    Gaston Rébuffat
                        Starlight and Storm, 1954, p. 20.

33 The man who bivouacs becomes one with the mountain.
    Gaston Rébuffat
                                                    Ibid., p. 27.

34 It is a noble folly, this climbing to a height . . .
    Guido Rey
    Quoted by J. Hubert Walker.
            Mountain Days in the Highlands and Alps, 1937, p. 198.

35 To myself, mountains are the beginning and the end of all
    natural scenery; in them, and in the forms of inferior landscape
    that lead to them, my affections are wholly bound up; . . .
    John Ruskin
    'The Hope of the Hills', in R. L. G. Irving (ed.), *The Mountain
                                                            Way:
                An Anthology in Prose and Verse, 1938, p. 14.

36 To climb with a friend is a pleasure; to climb alone is an education.
Count Henry Russel (Attributed)
Quoted by Walter Larden.
Recollections of An Old Mountaineer, 1910, p. 7.

37 Snow mountains are seldom friendly. Sometimes they seem to smile, but their welcome, for all its glitter, is treacherous and cruel.
Michael T. H. Sadler
'An Artist of Mountains', in Arnold H. M. Lunn (ed.),
Oxford Mountaineering Essays, 1912, p. 5.

38 The Alps are more than a gymnasium for their lover. Always alluring though they flout you; always lovely though they frown upon you; always dear though they slay you; they give you strength and friends and happiness, and to have known and loved them is indeed a liberal education.
Sir Claud Schuster
Quoted by J. Hubert Walker.
Mountain Days in the Highlands and Alps, 1937, p. 119.

39 Mountaineering, even of the humblest sort, satisfies two of the most deeply seated instincts of men – the desire to get to the top and the appetite for a little mild discomfort.
Sir Claud Schuster
Ibid., p. 144.

40 There is something fine in the desire to test human endurance against the deadening power of altitude . . .
Eric Shipton
Blank on the Map, 1938, p. 15.

41 Whether people realise that mountaineering is an inspiration, or condemn it as an insane risk of human life, it is obvious that its value lies in the motives of the climber.
Eric Shipton
Ibid.

42 A full appreciation of mountains is not to be experienced by merely looking; that is why men climb.
F. S. Smythe
Climbs and Ski Runs:
Mountaineering and Ski-ing in the Alps,
Great Britain and Corsica, 1930, p. 301.

43 Climb mountains from a centre if you will, but consummate
    your love for the hills by wandering across them.
    F. S. Smythe
                          Over Tyrolese Hills, 1936, preface, p. xv.

44 Such a question as, 'Why do you climb mountains?' is only
    answerable in terms of concrete experience and the expressible
    thoughts that permeate such experience; and when that experi-
    ence is transcendental and made up of many parts, just as white
    light is made up of many colours, the task of translating into
    words more than a tithe of its beauty becomes impossible.
    F. S. Smythe
                          The Spirit of the Hills, 1935, preface, p. xi.

45 Mountaineering is a search for beauty.
    F. S. Smythe
                                      Ibid., preface, p. xii.

46 It is better for a man to climb, however deplorable his methods
    of climbing and his mental approach to climbing, than for him
    not to climb.
    F. S. Smythe
                                              Ibid., p. 68.

47 Mountains are climbed because they exercise a strong attraction
    upon a small percentage of mankind . . .
    Showell Styles
                          How Mountains Are Climbed, 1958, p. 8.

48 Scenically the position of the bivouac was very fine but residen-
    tially it was damnable.
    H. W. Tilman
                          The Ascent of Nanda Devi, 1937, p. 189.

49 An expedition that cannot organise itself on an ordinary sheet
    of notepaper is bound to suffer from the effects of too much
    organisation.
    H. W. Tilman
    Quoted by Showell Styles.
                          Mountains of The Midnight Sun, 1954, p. 1.

50 I have a feeling that most of us nowadays have become rather
    blasé about conquering Everest . . . it is easy to forget what a
    monumental challenge the entire operation is and how it calls

for very special reserves of courage, stamina, determination, utter dedication and sheer mountaineering skill.
H.R.H. The Prince of Wales
> Foreword in Jon Fleming and Ronald Faux,
> *Soldiers on Everest*, 1977.

51 Mountaineering is something more than healthy exercise: it is a sport, and a great one . . .
E. A. M. Wedderburn
> *Alpine Climbing on Foot and with Ski*,
> revised by C. Douglas Milner, 1954, p. 1.

52 Sporting mountaineering requires that the skill of the party be nicely matched against the defences of the route. If it is too easy, it is not sport: if it is too hard, it is not pleasure.
E. A. M. Wedderburn
> Ibid.

53 Solitary climbing has terrible charms; with its devotees it becomes a vice.
E. A. M. Wedderburn
> Ibid., p. 6.

54 If Mr Gladstone could only have managed to attain to the summit of Snowdon he might have seen more than the coast of Ireland.
George Wherry
> *Alpine Notes and the Climbing Foot*, 1896, p. 67.

55 Truly it may be said that the outside of a mountain is good for the inside of a man.
George Wherry
> Ibid., p. 68.

56 . . . the foot, like the hand, is all adapted for climbing.
George Wherry
> Ibid., p. 121.

57 Climbing will not be less enjoyed by men possessing knowledge of the dangers . . . successful expeditions are made by those who understand such matters best, and look on their knowledge as an essential part of the sport.
George Wherry
> Ibid., p. 165.

58 After forty, a climber is in the old age of his youth, and must not be so reckless as to pace; his endurance and sure-footedness may be better, but his elasticity is less . . .
    George Wherry

Ibid., p. 166.

59 One man may be born a lover of the mountains, another by climbing come to love them later; but as a baby, boy, or man, he is always a climbing animal.
    George Wherry

Ibid.

60 Toil he must who goes mountaineering, but out of the toil comes strength (not merely muscular energy – more than that, an awakening of all the faculties), and from the strength arises pleasure.
    Edward Whymper

Scrambles among the Alps (1871), 1981, p. 161.

61 Do nothing in haste, look well to each step, and from the beginning think what may be the end.
    Edward Whymper

Ibid., p. 162.

62 When a man who is not a born mountaineer gets upon the side of a mountain, he speedily finds out that walking is an art . . .
    Edward Whymper

The Ascent of the Matterhorn, 1880, p. vii.

63 We who go mountain-scrambling have constantly set before us the superiority of fixed purpose of perseverance to brute force.
    Edward Whymper

Ibid., p. 296.

64 Climb if you will, but remember that courage and strength are nought without prudence, and that a momentary negligence may destroy the happiness of a lifetime.
    Edward Whymper

Ibid., p. 298.

65 Climbing calls for all that one has got in perseverance and endurance; but always the mountains give more than they demand; there is beauty and exaltation of spirit in abundance and peace that passes understanding.
Cicely Williams

Women on the Rope, 1973, p. 227.

66 The Alps have been and are, the cradle, the nursery, and the schoolroom of mountaineering . . .
Dr Claude Wilson
In Sidney Spencer (ed.), *The Londsdale Library*, vol. 18, p. 183.

67 The two places on earth on which tempests are most undesirable and most inconvenient are the ocean and the mountain; . . .
H. Schütz Wilson

Alpine Ascents and Adventures; or Rock and Snow Sketches, 1878, p. 195.

68 Of all mountains, the Matterhorn is the grandest and most terrible. Of all the mountains, the Weisshorn is the fairest and most feminine.
H. Schütz Wilson

Ibid., p. 315.

69 Walking is the main element of all the arts of mountaineering.
J. E. B. Wright
The Technique of Mountaineering, 1955, part 1, p. 11.

70 'Climbs' were in fact to us pre-existing, but concealed, lines of possibility contrived by nature and by time up steep and unknown cliffs.
Geoffrey Winthrop Young
Mountains With A Difference, 1953, p. 4.

71 . . . in a day of mountain climbing there are three strands twisted upon one another to make up a single length of experience, the things we are doing, the things we are seeing, and the things we are feeling.
Geoffrey Winthrop Young
On High Hills: Memories of the Alps, 1933, Foreword.

72   Mountains are a good adventure.
     Geoffrey Winthrop Young

                                                     Ibid., p. 360.

73   No mountaineer who respects common sense and mistrusts
     sentimentality will claim for mountain climbing that it is more,
     primarily, than a great sport – if perhaps the greatest. It is a
     high enough claim.
     Geoffrey Winthrop Young

                                                     Ibid., p. 362.

74   There is nothing of permanent value for our lives to be found
     ready-made and reach-me-down in mountain climbing, any
     more than in our other avocations or lasting pursuits.
     Geoffrey Winthrop Young

                                                     Ibid., p. 363.

75   . . . the value for a man of his every adventure depends as
     much upon what he may himself bring to it, of his own nature,
     as upon what the incidents or impressions of the unknown into
     which he is venturing may contribute.
     Geoffrey Winthrop Young

                                                            Ibid.

76   Mountaineering was a discovery
     Geoffrey Winthrop Young
                    'Mountain Prophets', in Walter Unsworth (ed.),
          Selections from the Alpine Journal, Peaks, Passes and Glaciers,
                                           1981, part 1, ch. 14.

77   In mountaineering there is only one principle: that we should
     secure on any given day the highest form of mountain adventure
     consistent with our sense of proportion. All else is more a
     matter of practice than of principle.
     Geoffrey Winthrop Young
     In Sidney Spencer (ed.), *The Lonsdale Library*, vol. 18, p. 40.

78   The hills are the opponents with whom we compete, not other
     climbers.
     Geoffrey Winthrop Young

                                                     Ibid., p. 44.

79   I have pierced them through and through. I have stood under their highest heights. I have faced their sternest precipices. I have traversed their greatest glaciers. I have visited their remotest peoples. For the mystery they wore I went among the mountains.
Sir Francis Younghusband
The Wonders of the Himalaya, 1924, p. 208.

COACHES/ COACHING

1   Coaching is 80% kidology.
Anonymous
Quoted by Dr N. Whitehead.
Conditioning for Sport, 1975, p. 25.

2   There is a syndrome in sports called 'paralysis by analysis'.
Arthur Ashe
Scholastic Coach, Sep., 1983, p. 18.

3   It is a fundamental premise of coaching that you can only work by consent, by the athlete's agreement to do what you ask. You have to have that. But the ultimate decision to go for something has to be the athlete's.
Peter Coe
The Times, Jan. 17, 1984.

4   In American society, it is commonly accepted that the success or failure of an athlete unit depends almost entirely upon the competence or incompetence of its coach.
Harry Edwards
Sociology of Sport, 1973, p. 137.

5 Do not be limited in your thinking. Being limited makes you predictable. If you are predictable you are vulnerable and being vulnerable makes you expendable.
Harry Gallagher
(Advice to Coaches)

Sprint the Crawl, 1976, p. 9.

6 To coach is to create and a thing of which to be proud.
Harry Gallagher

Ibid., p. 10.

7 Coaching is to inform, educate and encourage.
Gordon Jago

Football Coaching, 1974, p. 15.

8 Doing in sport is patterned and organized as are all experiences.
Francis W. Keenan
'The Concept of Doing', in R. G. Osterhoudt (ed.),
The Philosophy of Sport: A Collection of Original Essays,
1973, p. 141.

9 The football coach has become much more than another functionary of sport. He is expected to embody the very deepest of Americans' perceptions of themselves. He is expected to be authoritative, tough but fair, philosophical but imbued with a hunger for action. Ideally, he is a soldier-priest.
James Lawton
The All American War Game, 1984, p. 93.

10 The first aim of coaching is to improve an athlete's performance to a degree which would have been impossible for the athlete to have achieved by his own endeavours.
Tom McNab
Action: British Journal of Physical Education,
vol. 12, no. 4, Jul., 1981, p. 99.

11 Every game has problems. Understanding them and planning ways to overcome them is at the very centre of coaching.
Mike Williams
Rugby Sevens, 1975, p. 23.

COMPETITIONS

1 There is something in the Olympics, indefinable, springing
  from the soul, that must be preserved.
  Christopher Brasher
  Mexico 1968: A Diary of the XIXth Olympiad, 1968, p. 20.

2 The primary aim of the organisers of sports or Olympic competitions is not sport for its own sake but sport for capitalist profit;
  or rather, their aim is capitalist profit through sport.
  Jean-Marie Brohm
  Sport – A Prison of Measured Time, 1978, p. 137.

3 The biggest problem today is that the Olympic Games have
  become so important that political people want to take control
  of them. Our only salvation is to keep free from politics.
  Avery Brundage
  'Scorecard', *Sports Illustrated*, Jun. 8, 1964, p. 23.

4 Citius, Altius, Fortius.
  Reverend Father Didon (Attributed).
  (Olympic Motto)
  Quoted by David Guiney.
  The Dunlop Book of the Olympics, 1975.

5 The Modern Olympic Games symbolize the struggle between
  man's ideals and the reality within which he must live.
  Richard Espy
  The Politics of the Olympic Games, 1979, p. vii.

6 Nationalism was never a stranger to the Olympics.
  Richard Espy
  Ibid., p. 49.

7 The Olympics must be seen for what they are, for what they
  possess, rather than for what they hope to achieve.
  Richard Espy
  Ibid., p. 173.

8 Murphy's Law and Parkinson's Law have both contributed to
   an Olympics Law which says that the bigger a thing becomes,
   the more problems it attracts and the sooner it hastens its own
   demise.
   Norman Harris
                              The Sunday Times, Aug. 12, 1984.

9 The desire for international competition is not confined to the
   richer and more highly developed countries but is shared by
   those countries which might be thought to be preoccupied with
   the basic needs for survival.
   P. C. McIntosh
                              Sport in Society, 1963, p. 197.

10 People understand contests. You take a bunch of kids throwing
   rocks at random and people look askance, but if you go and
   hold a rock-throwing contest – people understand that.
   Don Murray
   Quoted by Gilbert Rogin.
                         Sports Illustrated, Oct. 18, 1965, p. 108.

11 And, if we thrive promise them such rewards
   As victors wear at the Olympian games.
   William Shakespeare
                    (George), *The Third Part of King Henry the Sixth*,
                                        act II, sc. III, l. 52.

CRICKET

1 A dirty look is the only acceptable expression of dissent, and
   we don't even like that.
   Anonymous
   (Cricket Umpire)
                    'Inside Track', *The Sunday Times*, Aug. 22, 1982.

2   In Affectionate Remembrance
of
ENGLISH CRICKET
WHICH DIED AT THE OVAL
on
29th AUGUST, 1882
Deeply lamented by a large circle of sorrowing
friends and acquaintances.

_____
R.I.P.
_____

N.B. – The body will be cremated and the
ashes taken to Australia.
Anonymous
Sporting Times, Sep. 2, 1882.
Quoted by Stephen Murray-Smith.
The Dictionary of Australian Quotations, 1984, p. 244.

3 Others scored faster; hit the ball harder; more obviously
murdered bowling. No one else, though, ever batted with more
consummate skill than his, which was based essentially on an
infallible sympathy with the bowled ball.
John Arlott
(On Jack Hobbs)
Jack Hobbs: Profile of 'The Master', 1982, p. 12.

4 He sometimes carried modesty to the length of humility; he felt
that he was lacking in profundity; but he was unquestionably a
good man.
John Arlott
(On Jack Hobbs)
Ibid., p. 16.

5 Cricket is a game in which attack and defence need to be nicely
balanced, but with a tendency to attack. It is often right for
one side to attack and the other to defend, often right for both
sides to attack. What can never be right is . . . for both sides
to defend.
R. L. Arrowsmith
A History of County Cricket: Kent, 1971, p. 157.

6 Ability alone is not enough. The ranks of discarded professionals are littered with batsmen who through nervousness have failed to translate their skill into runs and bowlers who have possessed everything except heart.
T. Bailey
Championship Cricket: A Review of County Cricket since 1945, 1961, p. 9.

7 Half the charm of cricket is its ever changing patterns.
T. Bailey
Ibid., p. 214.

8 It was 'not cricket' it was sports biz.
William J. Baker
(On World Series Cricket)
Sport in the Western World, 1982, p. 329.

9 The traditional dress of the Australian cricketer is the baggy green cap on the head and the chip on the shoulder. Both are ritualistically assumed.
Simon Barnes
The Times, May 9, 1985.

10 Cricket is a batsman's game.
Richie Benaud
Way of Cricket, 1961, p. 42.

11 In the Age of Austerity, Miller was a throwback to an earlier time; the quintessential romantic rebel.
Mihir Bose
Keith Miller: A Cricketing Biography, 1979, p. 4.

12 There is probably a greater premium on temperament for a batsman than for any player in any branch of sport.
Sir Donald Bradman
The Art of Cricket, 1958, p. 216.

13 May cricket continue to flourish and spread its wings. The world can only be richer for it.
Sir Donald Bradman
Ibid., p. 239.

14 The captain of a county cricket team is, all at once, managing
director, union leader, and pit-face worker.
J. M. Brearley
'Some Thoughts About Modern Captaincy',
Wisden: Cricketers' Almanack, 1982, p. 109.

15 There are three separate domains of captaincy; the technical
(or tactical), the psychological and the administrative. These
areas overlap.
J. M. Brearley
Ibid., p. 115.

16 Boycott and controversy have shared the longest opening part-
nership in the game.
Terry Brindle
'Geoffrey Boycott', *Wisden: Cricketers' Almanack*, 1978,
p. 140.

17 The fact that cricket has to be left off during the winter months
may be the reason for the fatality which seems to attend
professional cricketers; they seldom live long . . .
James Cantlie
Physical Efficiency, 1906, p. 199.

18 If a cricketer's mind and every nerve are awake and all his wits,
there can be no dullness, whether the scorers are active or not.
Neville Cardus
A Fourth Innings with Cardus, 1981, p. 12.

19 Cricket is wearisome and sterile only when the minds of the
players are wearisome and sterile, or when the prize, the aggre-
gates and records, render impulses of sport null and void.
Neville Cardus
Ibid., p. 23.

20 There ought to be some other means of reckoning quality in
this the best and loveliest of games; the scoreboard is an ass.
Neville Cardus
Ibid., p. 109.

21 The laws of cricket tell of the English love of compromise
between a particular freedom and a general orderliness, or
legality.
Neville Cardus
Sir Rupert Hart-Davis (ed.), *Cardus on Cricket*, 1977, p. 19.

22 Cricket more than any other game is inclined towards sentimentalism and cant.
    Neville Cardus

Ibid., p. 112.

23 The umpire at cricket is like the geyser in the bathroom; we cannot do without it, yet we notice it only when it is out of order.
    Neville Cardus

Ibid., p. 147.

24 Like the British Constitution, cricket was not made: it has 'grown'.
    Neville Cardus

English Cricket, 1945, p. 7.

25 It is far more than a game, this cricket.
    Neville Cardus

Ibid., p. 9.

26 The history of cricket, made by Englishmen no more ethical than jockeys and pugilists and footballers, does justice like a play or a pageant to our national horse-sense, sentiment and powers of accommodation.
    Neville Cardus

Ibid.

27 The elements are cricket's presiding geniuses.
    Neville Cardus

Ibid., p. 17.

28 There is scope at cricket for men to reveal themselves.
    Neville Cardus

Ibid.

29 I like to think about time and I like cricket. The two likings are possibly not inconsistent.
    Marvin Cohen
        'The Time Factor', in Allen Synge (ed.), *Strangers' Gallery: Some Foreign Views of English Cricket*, 1974, p. 26.

30 Life is an elaborate metaphor for cricket.
    Marvin Cohen

Ibid., p. 59.

31 Is there life after cricket?
Marvin Cohen

Ibid., p. 70.

32 On the plains of India, in Australia (as some of our English cricketers have learnt to their cost), in Egypt, wherever Englishmen go, there cricket finds a home and a hearty welcome.
P. H. Ditchfield
Old English Sports: Pastimes and Customs (1891), 1975, p. 61.

33 There is a widely held and quite erroneous belief that cricket is just another game.
H.R.H. The Duke of Edinburgh
'The Pleasures of Cricket', *Wisden: Cricketers' Almanack*, 1975, p. 67.

34 Watching cricket without Wisden is almost as unthinkable as batting without pads.
H.R.H. The Duke of Edinburgh

Ibid.

35 Any detached observer has reluctantly to admit that most of what passes for top-level cricket today is the wrong kind of cricket played by the wrong kind of cricketer to titillate the wrong kind of spectator.
H. A. Harris
Sport in Britain: Its Origins and Development, 1975, p. 78.

36 As harrowing occupations go, there can't be much to choose between the Australian cricket captaincy and social work on skid row.
Doug Ibbotson
Sporting Scenes, 1980, p. 45.

37 To get down to hard facts, cricket matches are won by runs and not by style.
G. L. Jessop
A Cricketer's Log, 1922, p. 255.

38 League cricket is club cricket spiced by competition and streamlined by rules and regulations.
John Kay
Cricket in the Leagues, 1970, intro.

39 Overthrows are outside the necessities of cricket but they do
sometimes augment the enjoyment of the game.
J. M. Kilburn
> *Overthrows: A Book of Cricket*, 1975, preface.

40 Overthrows have a dubious standing in the accountancy of
cricket.
J. M. Kilburn
> Ibid.

41 Cricketing days remembered are coloured by the weather.
J. M. Kilburn
> Ibid., p. 57.

42 Cricket is a team game of individual encounter.
J. M. Kilburn
> Ibid., p. 96.

43 Cricket shares with Cleopatra the charm of infinite variety.
J. M. Kilburn
> Ibid., p. 129.

44 Herbert Sutcliffe was one of the great cricketers and he brought
to cricket as to all his undertakings an assurance and capacity
for concentration that positively commanded success.
J. M. Kilburn
> In *Wisden: The Cricketers' Almanack*, 1979.

45 Bowling
   1. Should you desire to bowl leg-breaks, close the right eye.
   2. Off-breaks are obtained by closing the left eye.
   3. To bowl straight, close both.
Jos A. Knowlson
> 'The Lady Cricketer's Guide', *Punch*, Aug. 29, 1906.

46 In cricket it has always been hard to say goodbye. 'I read of
my dismissal in the papers' has been a frequent cri de coeur.
Robin Marler
> *The Sunday Times*, Jul. 24, 1983, p. 32.

47 It is no sinecure being the son of a famous sportsman.
Dudley Nourse
> *Cricket in the Blood*, 1949, p. 11.

48 Every innings has its own thrill, every game its own individuality.
Dudley Nourse

Ibid., p. 206.

49 He who strokes the ball with loving care is a gentleman. He who studies it with hawk eyes is a worried man. He who blocks fast bowlers and belts spinners is a wise man.
Peter Roebuck
Slices of Cricket, 1982, p. 16.

50 For as long as we continue to play cricket, and this surely will be linked with eternity, the name of Jack Hobbs will stand immortal . . .
Gordon Ross
A History of County Cricket: Surrey, 1971, p. 153.

51 Gilbert Laird Jessop, the Rupert of the cricket field . . .
Rowland Ryder
'Gilbert Jessop – The Most Exciting Cricketer of Them All',
Wisden: Cricketers' Almanack, 1972, p. 42.

52 I have been classed as a 'rebel' and even a 'misfit' by many people in authority. But not a rebel for the hell of it. Not a misfit for the sake of being different.
John Snow
Cricket Rebel: An Autobiography, 1976, p. 3.

53 A fast bowler who doesn't get results has no future.
John Snow
Quoted by B. V. Easterbrook.
Wisden: Cricketers' Almanack, 1973, p. 75.

54 The truest of all axioms about cricket is that the game is as good as those who play it.
E. W. Swanton
Sort of a Cricket Person, 1972, p. 304.

55 The situation of the cricketer is similar to that of man himself, uncomfortably alone in a strangely unapplauding universe, for all his glorious achievements.
Allen Synge
Strangers' Gallery: Some Foreign Views of English Cricket (ed.),
1974, p. 14.

56   No one who is not prepared to do his best to become a good fielder has the right to call himself a cricketer.
                    The MCC Cricket Coaching Book, 1976, p. 3.

57   Perhaps the most important of all cricket truths which a coach can instil is that fielding is fun, and infinitely more fun if everyone tries.
                                                       Ibid.

58   The bowler must constantly remind himself that the initiative lies with him, and that he must do everything he can to retain it.
                                              Ibid., p. 29.

59   Every batsman must realize that his duty is first, last, and all the time to his side and not to himself.
                                              Ibid., p. 73.

60   Like all cricket devotees I have many, many times shared with all around me that infectious, 'breathless hush' tension as a batsman, however well-set, however self-possessed, has to face up to the obligation of scoring that hundredth run.
     Ben Travers
                    94 Declared Cricket Reminiscences, 1981, p. 22.

61   The really great batsmen fall into two categories. One comes to the wicket saying to the bowlers 'I am going to slaughter you'. The other comes to the wicket saying 'You can't get me out'.
     Ben Travers
                                              Ibid., p. 73.

62   The only bowler who ever got to be a knight was Sir Francis Drake.
     Ben Travers
                                              Ibid., p. 75.

63   If there is any game in the world that attracts the half-baked theorist more than cricket I have yet to hear of it.
     Freddie Trueman
                    Freddie Trueman's Book of Cricket, 1964, p. 7.

64 I have never believed in making life easier for batsmen.
Freddie Trueman

Ibid., p. 41.

65 The difference between a fast bowler and a good fast bowler is
not extra muscle but extra brains.
Freddie Trueman

Ibid., p. 43.

66 A cricket match may be likened to a battle, for there are, as in
warfare, only three possible results – victory, defeat, or an
indecisive encounter.
P. F. Warner
   'Captaincy', in P. F. Warner (ed.), *Cricket A New Edition*,
   Badminton Library of Sports and Pastimes, 1920, p. 120.

67 Length, the foundation of all bowling, is not a natural gift.
E. R. Wilson
'Bowling', in P. F. Warner (ed.).

Ibid., p. 56.

68 Spin alas! is natural.
E. R. Wilson

Ibid., p. 58.

CROQUET

1 Croquet is not Golf Croquet.
E. P. C. Cotter

Tackle Croquet This Way, 1960, p. 13.

2 (Golf Croquet) has as much relation to Croquet as Cork Pool
has to Billiards . . .
E. P. C. Cotter

Ibid.

3   . . . the fact that the aged can play the game should be a source
of gratitude to all and not a departure-point for derision.
E. P. C. Cotter

Ibid., p. 15.

4   Handicap Doubles are the factor X of Croquet. There is much
to be said for them, much to be said against.
E. P. C. Cotter

Ibid., p. 121.

5   To peg out, or not to peg out – that is the question . . .
J. W. Solomon

Croquet, 1966, p. 71.

CURLING

1   Frae Maidenkirk to John O'Groats
Nae curlers like the clergy.
Anonymous
(Old proverb)
Quoted by Robin Welsh.

Beginner's Guide to Curling, 1969, p. 166.

2   It is the broom that wins the battle.
Reverend John Kerr
Quoted by Robin Welsh.

Ibid., p. 95.

3   The object of the player is to lay his stone as near to the mark
as possible, to guard that of his partner, which had been well
laid before, or to strike off that of his antagonist.
Thomas Pennant

A Tour of Scotland, 1772.

Quoted by W. H. Murray.

The Curling Companion, 1981.

4   Curling lifts the spirit and captivates the mind.
Robin Welsh

Beginner's Guide to Curling, 1969, p. 40.

5 Conceit is a word we don't like in curling but the value of self-confidence cannot be stressed too strongly.
Robin Welsh

Ibid., p. 124.

6 There are keen golfers, keen shinty players, keen anglers. But only curlers are 'Keen Keen'.
Robin Welsh

Ibid., p. 173.

CYCLING

1 In a space age increasingly subject to the threats of noise, excessive speed, and pollution, there is still a significant place for the balanced wheel.
Frederick Alderson

Bicycling: A History, 1972, p. 205.

2 The first race probably took place as soon as the second bicycle was completed.
J. Else

'The A–Z of Cycling', (b) 'The Sport', Paper presented at *Cycling A New Deal – Report of a Conference held at Nottingham, Nov. 24, 1978.*

3 The route of the Tour de France is different each year, but always based on the same two principles – tradition and solvency – and the same four landmarks: the Alps, the Pyrenees, the Massif Central and Paris.
Geoffrey Nicholson

The Great Bike Race, 1977, p. 31.

4 Nearly all the tactics of cycle racing are based on a simple mechanical principle; that all else being equal, two men who take it in turn to pace each other will travel further and faster than a man riding on his own.
Geoffrey Nicholson

Ibid., p. 74.

5 A fast car is a fast car whoever is at the wheel, which isn't to
deny the driver's contribution. But on a bike the cyclist is both
the driver and the engine.
Geoffrey Nicholson

Ibid., p. 138.

DIVING

1 Springboard diving is a unique activity, a combination of
aquatics and acrobatics.
C. J. Alderson

Selected Aquatic Articles, 1964, p. 6.

2 Springboard diving is the art and science of propelling the body
up into the air and coming down into the water from a 75 to
90 degree angle on either end of the body.
C. J. Alderson

Ibid.

3 Complexity in diving begins with the springboard.
Anne Ross Fairbanks

Teaching Springboard Diving, 1964, p. 2.

4 Ultimately the champion will win by beautiful execution rather
than by mere verve.
Wally Orner

'Diving', in *The Official Coaching Book of the E.S.S.A.* (ed.),
Swimming and Diving, 1972, p. 65.

5 There is a world of difference between what the diver thinks
he is doing and what he is in fact doing.
Wally Orner

Ibid., p.71

DRAMA/
ENTERTAINMENT

1 At its best, sport is living drama.
John Bromley

> *The Observer*, Aug. 22, 1982.

2 Like artists and achievers of every kind, successful athletes
must be, at a minimum, four things: gifted, hungry, intelligent
and toughminded.
E. H. Cady

> *The Big Game: College Sports and American Life*, 1978,
> p. 146.

3 Sport and art imitate and re-create a perceived order moving
from improvised representation to more intricately designed
expression, from a child's make-believe to drama, from a stum-
bling skip rope reaction to rhythm to poetry and ballet, from
the kinetic pleasure of body movement to a baseball game.
Ron Cummings

> 'Double Play and Replay:
> Living out there in Television Land',
> *Journal of Popular Culture*, 1974/75.

4 The game is so full of plot – interest and drama.
C. B. Fry
(On Rugby Union)

> Preface in E. H. D. Sewell, *Rugger: The Man's Game*,
> revised by O. L. Owen, 1950.

5 American professional sport has never had any doubts that it is
part of the entertainment industry, competing with the likes of
the movies, the travel industry and the theatre for a share of
the leisure dollar.
Paul Gardner

> *Nice Guys Finish Last: Sport and American Life*, 1974, p. 22.

6 Sport is not like a novel or a play, with the ending already
decided. It is alive and dynamic.
Angela Patmore

> *Playing On Their Nerves: The Sport Experiment*, 1979, p. 8.

7 If the connection between the 'new' theatre and baseball once
   seemed tenuous, recent trends in the theatre . . . trends such
   as Happenings, Action Theatre, Game Theatre, Ray Gun
   Theatre etc. . . . have now rendered the distinction between
   sport and theatre, between theatre and baseball, obsolete.
   Louis Phillips
   'The Mets and the New Theatre', *Journal of Popular Culture*,
                                vol. II, no. 2, Fall, 1968, p. 481.

8 Sport has achieved its position in the entertainment world by
   commercialisation and the emphasis on performance.
   Richard Thompson
                                    Race and Sport, 1964, p. 3.

9 Pain raises sport from the level of entertainment to that of
   human achievement . . .
   L. Pearce Williams
                            The New York Times, Oct. 23, 1977.

EQUESTRIANISM/ RIDING

1 And first thou shalt knowe that a good horse hath I (i.e. 50)
   propertyes, that is to say ii of a man, ii of a badger, iv of a lyon,
   ix of an oxe, ix of a hare, ix of a foxe, viii of an asse and viii of
   a woman.
   Anonymous
   Quoted by Dorian Williams.
                        The Horseman's Companion, 1967, p. 109.

2 Here's to that bundle of sentient nerves with the heart of a
   woman, the eye of a gazelle, the courage of a gladiator, and
   the proud obedience of a soldier – The Horse!
   Anonymous
   (Ancient Toast)
   Quoted by Col. Harry Llewellyn.
                    The Whitbread Book of Horses, 1962, intro.

3   Never look a gift horse in the mouth.
Anonymous
(Traditional Proverb)
Quoted by Rintoul Booth.
The Horseman's Handbook to end all Horseman's Handbooks,
1975, p. 62.

4   I was formed by nature for a good seat on a horse, and without
a good seat a man cannot have good hands.
'Avon'
How I Became a Sportsman, 1888, p. 47.

5   In spite of his taste for throwing Christians to lions, Caligula
loved horses and was therefore basically all right.
Rintoul Booth
The Horseman's Handbook to end all Horseman's Handbooks,
1975, p. 15.

6   Galloping is a sort of over-excited canter.
Rintoul Booth
Ibid., p. 37.

7   The seat on a horse makes gentlemen of some and grooms of
others.
Cervantes
Don Quixote.
Quoted by Rintoul Booth.
Ibid., p. 33.

8   Gold medals aren't given out with the oats and the bran in this
game.
Hugh McIlvanney
(On Equestrianism – Three Day Event)
The Observer, Jul. 29, 1984, p. 34.

9   Anybody can learn to ride, for riding is nothing but skill.
W. Müseler
Riding Logic, translated by F. W. Schiller (1937), 1975, intro.

10   Feel is no black magic, and anybody can acquire it to a consider-
able degree.
W. Müseler
Ibid.

11 Riding is pleasant and can be made an art. And who would not
be an artist?
W. Müseler

Ibid.

12 The training of the rider comprises three things: seat, feeling
and influence.
W. Müseler

Ibid., p. 1.

13 All difficulties begin with the command 'trot on' . . .
W. Müseler

Ibid., p. 13.

14 To ride well, one must enjoy it; though those who enjoy it do
not necessarily ride well.
Diane R. Tuke

The Rider's Handbook, 1977, p. 7.

15 Badminton is to horse trials what Lord's is to cricket.
Sheila Willcox

Introduction in Barbara Cooper,
Badminton: The Three-Day Event 1949–1969, 1969.

16 The one best precept – the golden rule in dealing with a horse
– is never to approach him angrily.
Xenophon (365 BC)
Quoted by Dorian Williams.

The Horseman's Companion, 1967, p. 105.

EQUIPMENT

1 For everyone the ball provides a means of relaxing, forgetting
about everyday cares, strengthening one's body, enjoying
movement . . .
Anonymous

Sport in the USSR, Dec., 1981, p. 3.

2 Without doubt, the single most important object in sport is the ball.
Andrew Bailey

Future Sport, 1982, p. 58.

3 The evolution of the ball is always limited by the nature of the bat.
A. E. Crawley

The Book of the Ball, 1913, p. 64.

4 The ball is neutral in all respects
K. Privalor

Sport in the USSR, Dec., 1981, p. 30.

FENCING

1 Fencing is a sport of perception and intuition as well as one of technique.
Bob Anderson

All About Fencing, 1970, p. 6.

2 The qualities required of the complete swordsman are, on the physical side, technique, speed and stamina; mentally, he must possess judgment, opportuneness; and morally, perseverance.
Léon Bertrand

The Fencer's Companion, 1935, part 1, section 1, p. 1.

3 Fencing is of such lasting interest precisely because the discipline of muscular and reflex actions acquired by intensive practice is secondary to the mental analysis of the opponent's reactions and the devising of strategy and tactics to outwit him.
C-L. de Beaumont

Your Book of Fencing, 1970, p. 14.

4 Only the impatient person cannot fence.
Henry De Silva

British Journal of Physical Education, vol. 2, no. 5, Sep., 1971, p. 71.

5 The nature of fencing is simple enough. Fencing is fighting.
   Albert Manley

   Complete Fencing, 1979, p. 3.

6 My conviction is that épéeists are born, not made.
   Albert Manley

   Ibid., p. 200.

7 A Master of Arms is more honourable than a Master of Arts,
   for good fighting came before good writing.
   Marston (1617)
   Quoted by J. D. Aylward.

   The English Master of Arms:
   From The Twelfth to the Twentieth Century, 1956.

8 . . . sword against sword, ourselves alone.
   William Shakespeare

   (Antony), *Antony and Cleopatra*, act III, sc. XI, l. 27.

9 . . . he will fence with his own shadow.
   William Shakespeare

   (Portia), *The Merchant of Venice*, act I, sc. II, l. 65.

10 Alas, Sir! I cannot fence.
    William Shakespeare

    (Rugby), *The Merry Wives of Windsor*, act II, sc. III, l. 15.

11 To be successful in any sport from soccer to horse-racing, from
    gliding to golf, needs brain as well as physical skill; neither is
    much use without the other; and I think fencing demonstrates
    this more fully than any other sport.
    Gillian Sheen

    Instructions to Young Fencers, 1958, p. 12.

12 The sabre offers a larger arsenal of movements than the foil or
    épée. It is perhaps the most emotional type of fencing, and it
    has the most spectator appeal.
    L. Shishkin

    Sport in the USSR, Jan., 1982, p. 5.

13 Fencing is like playing chess with a sword in your hand!
    Valentina Sidorova

    Sport in the USSR, Oct., 1978, p. 23.

FIELD SPORTS

1 Fox-Hunting, however lively and animating it may be in the field, is but a dull, dry subject to write upon; and I can now assure you from experience, that it is much less difficult to follow a fox-chase than to describe one.
Peter Beckford

> *Thoughts on Hunting:*
> *In a series of Familiar Letters to a Friend*
> (1899), 1951, letter XIV, p. 115.

2 You tell me, I should always kill a fox: I might answer, I must catch him first.
Peter Beckford

> Ibid.

3 There is infinite pleasure in hearing a fox well found.
Peter Beckford

> Ibid., letter XIV, p. 120.

4 . . . fox-hunting is a kind of warfare; its uncertainties, its fatigues, its difficulties, and its dangers, rendering it interesting above all other diversions.
Peter Beckford

> Ibid., letter XVII, p. 135.

5 Never had fox or hare the honour of being chased to death by so accomplished a hunter; never was a huntsman's dinner graced with such urbanity and wit. He would bag a fox in Greek, find a hare in Latin, inspect his kennels in Italian, and direct the economy of his stables in French.
Sir Egerton Brydges
(On Peter Beckford)
Quoted by J. Otho Paget.

> Introduction to Peter Beckford, *Thoughts on Hunting:*
> *In a series of Familiar Letters to a Friend*
> (1899), 1951, p. xi.

6 On what Horse can we venture our lives more securely than
   on the Hunter?
   Nicholas Cox
   Quoted by Rintoul Booth.
   > *The Horseman's Handbook to end all Horseman's*
   > *Handbooks*, 1975, p. 133.

7 To an Englishman sport is as the salt of life – particularly the
   field sports of country life.
   F. W. Hackwood
   > *Old English Sports*, 1907, p. 23.

8 He did not know that a keeper is only a poacher turned outside
   in, and a poacher a keeper turned inside out.
   Charles Kingsley
   > *The Water Babies*, ch. 1.

9 The definition of the word 'Sport' is the taking of a wild animal
   in such a way that the said animal has a fair chance of escape.
   H. Langford Brown
   > *The Water's Side*, 1926, p. 1.

10 Regard shooting as a means to an end and not an end in itself.
   John Marchington
   > *The Complete Shot*, 1981, inside cover.

11 All sensitive sportsmen will share my reservations about the
   act of killing, but we all face the same great anomaly – that
   without the hunt and the kill the whole essence of the sport
   would disappear.
   John Marchington
   > Ibid., p. 8.

12 That men are attracted by guns is beyond dispute; what is less
   clear is why.
   John Marchington
   > Ibid., p. 9.

13 Fieldcraft begins with an attitude of mind and while the
   different aspects can be taught and learnt, it comes more readily
   to some than others.
   John Marchington
   > Ibid., p. 56.

14 Tracing the history of wildfowling is not unlike exploring the moon – one part is permanently dark and the other constantly light.
John Marchington
The History of Wildfowling, 1980, p. 77.

15 Punt-gunning as a sport had everything a manly man could desire – a big, very big, gun; personal command of a salt-water craft, with all the thrills and dangers of sea; an arduous demanding activity to test one's endurance and character; the occasional great triumph and all the romance of ordinary wild-fowling multiplied by the circumstances.
John Marchington
Ibid., p. 163.

16 The ever-changing pattern of our field sports is like a carpet, now bright, now dark, in places tattered or holed, but with vivid new patches here and there.
J. K. Stanford
The Complex Gun, 1968, p. 16.

17 The English country gentleman galloping after a fox – the unspeakable in full pursuit of the uneatable.
Oscar Wilde
A Woman of No Importance, act 1.

FITNESS/HEALTH

1 You're not old until it takes you longer to rest up than it does to get tired.
Dr Phog Allen (Aged 79)
'Scorecard', *Sports Illustrated*, Sep. 6, 1965, p. 12.

2 Death is the final penalty, but the life of a sportsman on drugs is a perpetual living penalty because he is offending against himself.
Christopher Brasher
The Observer, Jun. 11, 1978.

3 No form of exercise is complete in which the lower limbs do not play the chief part.
James Cantlie
Physical Efficiency, 1906, p. 161.

4 It is exercise alone that supports the spirits and keeps the mind in vigour.
Cicero
Quoted by John Boyle O'Reilly.
Ethics of Boxing and Manly Sport, 1888.

5 Intellectual progress is conditioned at every step by bodily vigor.
Comenius
Quoted by Charles A. Bucher.
Foundations of Physical Education, 1964, p. 263.

6 I'm not an anarchist, but I guess I'd like to start an aerobic revolution.
Kenneth H. Cooper
Aerobics, 1968, p. 160.

7 Fitness might be defined as the degree of adaptation to the stressors of a given lifestyle.
Frank Dick
Training Theory, 1978, p. 35.

8 The health of the people is the foundation upon which all their happiness and all their powers as a state depend.
Benjamin Disraeli
Quoted by Charles A. Bucher.
Foundations of Physical Education, 1964, p. 107.

9 It should be noted that the drug problem will not leave sport of its own accord.
Russell Fleming
Action: British Journal of Physical Education,
vol. 12, no. 5, Sep., 1981, p. 132.

10 Regular vigorous exercise is not a panacea although it has many of the attributes of one.
Michael Freemantle
Slim for Life, 1980, p. 86.

11 There is no better preventive of nervous exhaustion than regular unhurried muscular exercise. If we could moderate our hurry, lessen our worry, and increase our open-air exercise, a large portion of nervous diseases would be abolished.
James Muir Howie
Quoted by John Boyle O'Reilly.
Ethics of Boxing and Manly Sport, 1888.

12 Our own history, perhaps better than the history of any other great country, vividly demonstrates the truth of the belief that physical vigor and health are essential accompaniments to the qualities of intellect and spirit on which a nation is built.
President John F. Kennedy
Sports Illustrated, Jul. 16, 1962, p. 12.

13 Calisthenics is not a dirty word.
Judy Lawson
'The Women's Problems', in Bob Fisher (ed.),
Crewing Racing Dinghies and Keelboats, 1976, p. 146.

14 Health, physical fitness and first-class sporting and athletic performance are not necessarily synonymous.
L. A. Liversedge
'Medical Aspects of Sport and Physical Fitness',
Paper presented at Manchester Statistical Society, Dec. 11, 1963.

15 Physical recreation should refresh and recreate the spirit.
Arthur S. MacNalty
Foreword in Board of Education Physical Training Series,
Recreation and Physical Fitness for Girls and Women,
no. 16, 1937.

16 Lack of activity destroys the good condition of every human being, while movement and methodical physical exercise save it and preserve it.
Plato
Quoted by Charles A. Bucher.
Foundations of Physical Education, 1964.

17 . . . if one is healthy, exercise is unnecessary, whilst if one is
ill it may be positively dangerous.
Professor Sir Robert Platt
(Former President of The Royal College of Physicians)
Quoted by L. A. Liversedge.
'Medical Aspects of Sport and Physical Fitness',
Paper presented at Manchester Statistical Society, Dec. 11,
1963.

18 Jogging is as natural as breathing.
Harcourt Roy
Jogging The Anytime Exercise, 1978, p. 10.

19 The greatest of follies is to sacrifice health for any other
advantage.
Schopenhauer
Quoted by Charles A. Bucher.
Foundations of Physical Education, 1964, p. 263.

20 Most recreational directors, physical education instructors, and
promoters of exercise-for-your-health programs feel much the
same as the fellow who finds it difficult to give away five-dollar
bills down Main Street. People just won't believe it's for real.
Dr George Sheehan
'Going Beyond Fitness', in The Editors of
Runner's World Magazine (ed.), *The Complete Runner*, 1974,
p. 2.

21 We do not yet sufficiently realize the truth that as, in this life
of ours, the physical underlies the mental, the mental must not
be developed at the expense of the physical.
Herbert Spencer
Quoted by Charles A. Bucher.
Foundations of Physical Education, 1964, p. 263.

22 There is no kind of exercise that has more uniformly met the
approbation of authors in general than running.
Joseph Strutt
The Sports and Pastimes of the People of England,
1830, book II, p. 77.

23 A man must often exercise or fast or take physic, or be sick.
Sir W. Temple
Quoted by John Boyle O'Reilly.
Ethics of Boxing and Manly Sport, 1888.

24 The vital thing about getting fit is getting started . . .
The Health Education Council

Looking After Yourself, 1980, p. 5.

25 Health consists of a rhythmic rise and fall, a kind of dance of
life. It is not static but full of movement, and it has to be re-
won, maintained and heightened daily, through the years and
decades, up to highest old age.
Ernest Von Aaken

Von Aaken Method, 1976, p. 12.

26 . . . beer is commendable, wine is acceptable and spirits are
damnable.
Dr J. G. P. Williams
(On alcohol and the athlete)
Quoted by L. A. Liversedge.

'Medical Aspects of Sport and Physical Fitness',
Paper presented at Manchester Statistical Society,
Dec. 11, 1963.

27 . . . what a disgrace it is for a man to grow old without ever
seeing the beauty of which his body is capable.
Xenophon
Quoted by Charles A. Bucher.

Foundations of Physical Education, 1964, p. 129.

28 The only possible form of exercise is to talk, not to walk.
Oscar Wilde
(In an interview)
Quoted by Alvin Redman.

The Epigrams of Oscar Wilde: An Anthology, 1952.

FOOTBALL
(ALL CODES)

1 Football, in all its varieties is pre-eminently a game of military
   tactics.
   A. E. Crawley
   The Book of the Ball, 1913, p. 184.

2 The tactical difference between Association Football and Rugby
   with its varieties seems to be that in the former the ball is the
   missile, in the latter men are the missiles.
   A. E. Crawley
   Ibid., p. 185.

3 A Welsh defeat at soccer or a Scottish defeat at Rugby can be
   treated by the local populations with relative shoulder-shrug-
   ging indifference, but for the Welsh to lose at Rugby or the
   Scots to lose at soccer is akin to a national disaster.
   B. Dobbs
   Edwardians at Play: Sport 1890–1914, 1973, p. 75.

4 Up, and by coach to Sir Ph. Warwickes, the street being full
   of foot-balls, it being a great frost.
   Samuel Pepys
   (Play being possible because the frost would have reduced the
   amount of horse-traffic)
   The Diary of Samuel Pepys, Jan. 3, 1665.

5 It has always seemed to me that one of the big differences
   between Rugby and soccer is the assumption that in Rugby the
   players will do their best to play to the laws; while in soccer
   the players follow the laws until it is to their advantage to break
   them . . .
   Derek Robinson
   Rugby World, vol. II, no. 3, Mar., 1971, p. 16.

6 . . . you base football player.
   William Shakespeare
   (Earl of Kent), *King Lear*, act I, sc. IV, l. 95.

FOOTBALL (AMERICAN)

1 Losing the Super Bowl is worse than death. You have to get up next morning.
George Allen
'Inside track', *The Sunday Times*, Jan. 22, 1984.

2 The algebra teacher used to be the football coach. Now the football coach is the algebra teacher.
Sammy Baugh
'Scorecard', *Sports Illustrated*, Jul. 2, 1962, p. 6.

3 Football is not a contact sport – it's a collision sport. Dancing is a contact sport.
Duffy Daugherty
'Scorecard', *Sports Illustrated*, Oct. 14, 1963, p. 14.

4 If a football player isn't tough as nails to begin with and in good, hard condition, he's flirting with a wheel-chair.
Wilfrid Diamond
This Guy Marciano, 1955, p. 16.

5 You can learn more character on the two-yard line than you can anywhere in life.
Paul Dietzel
Quoted by Rex Lardner.
Sports Illustrated, Nov. 26, 1962, p. 32.

6 College Football today is one of the last great strongholds of genuine old-fashioned American hypocrisy.
Paul Gallico
'Last Stronghold of Hypocrisy', in G. H. Sage (ed.),
Sport and American Society: Selected Readings (1938), 1970,
p. 111.

7 In the professional world, a black quarterback is decidedly a rara avis. A rather more common avis is the black cornerback.
Paul Gardner
Nice Guys Finish Last: Sport and American Life, 1974,
p. 150.

8 American Football is not so much a sport as a way of strife.
Doug Ibbotson

Sporting Scenes, 1980, p. 91.

9 They say football is America's greatest game, but it's not. The
greatest game in America is called opportunity. Football is
merely a great expression of it.
Joe Kapp
Quoted by James Lawton.

The All American War Game, 1984, p. 12.

10 Placekickers aren't football players. They're hired feet.
Alex Karras

'Coaches' Corner', *Scholastic Coach*, Apr. 1979.

11 American football is about many things. It is about great skill
and brute power, about American tradition and ambition and,
in a real sense, the way the world's richest, most self-indulgent
society sees itself. Most of all, American football is about
money.
James Lawton

The All American War Game, 1984, intro.

12 There is much to fascinate in the more sporting aspects of
gridiron football, in the character of the players and the tactics
of the coaching, but any understanding of it as a phenomenon
has to be informed by the fact that without television and
gambling it would today probably be just another game.
James Lawton

Ibid.

13 If all of sport is a magnificent triviality, American football seems
least tolerant of the limitation.
James Lawton

Ibid., p. 2.

14 Offense is the shop window of football. Defense is the heart
and the conscience and, often, the entrails.
James Lawton

Ibid., p. 123.

15 Championships are won on defense.
Vince Lombardi
Quoted by Tex Maule.
Sports Illustrated, no. 19, 1967, p. 30.

16 If the meek ever inherit the earth, our defensive line is going
to wind up owning Texas.
Jerry Moore
'Coaches' Corner', *Scholastic Coach*, Dec., 1982, p. 57.

17 Discipline represents a combination of what is imposed by the
coach and what is accepted by the player.
Darrell Mudra
Scholastic Coach, Aug., 1982, p. 34.

18 Every successful coach must have a successful quarterback.
Ara Parseghian
'Scorecard', *Sports Illustrated*, Nov. 30, 1964, p. 20.

19 We're looking forward to a great season at the University of
California – if we can find a way to put cleats on their sandals.
Ronald Reagan
'Scorecard', *Sports Illustrated*, Apr. 24, 1967, p. 20.

20 A football player has always been referred to as a football player.
He's not. He's a man who happens to play football.
Hank Stram
Quoted by Peter Richmond.
Miami Herald, Nov. 25, 1984.

21 There's no tougher way to make easy money than pro football.
Norm Van Brocklin
'Scorecard', *Sports Illustrated*, Oct. 23, 1967, p. 16.

22 Many an All-American has been made by a long run, a weak
defense, and a poet in the press box.
Robert Zuppke
'Coaches' Corner', *Scholastic Coach*, Dec., 1982.

FOOTBALL (ASSOCIATION)

1 When more people are talking soccer topics from one Saturday to the next instead of 'H' bombs, wars and politics, the country will be a better place to live in.
Henry Adamson
>*FA News: The Official Journal of the Football Association,*
>Jan., 1962, p. 208.

2 The struggle between defence and attack – the basic contest in football – is really, and always, the chief interest in any football: that is why a 'friendly' match never quite rings true.
John Arlott
>'The Appreciation of Football',
>in A. H. Fabian and Geoffrey Green (ed.), *Association
>Football*, 1960, vol. 2, p. 180.

3 There is no harder exercise in the appreciation of football than that of taking one's eye off the ball.
John Arlott
>Ibid., p. 189.

4 Football can be no more than a minor corner of any balanced life. Within that corner, however, it can be roundly satisfying.
John Arlott
>Ibid., p. 200.

5 Soccer is a man's game; not an outing for mamby-pambies.
J. Charlton
>*For Leeds and England,* 1967, p. 158.

6 The beauty has gone out of football . . . it has lost its poetry, its artistic gentleness . . .
Alfredo Di Stefano
Quoted by Matt D'Arcy.
>*Manchester Evening News,* Sep. 13, 1972.

7 When they sign a new player who plays in your position it is not funny.
Eamon Dunphy
Only a Game?: The Diary of a Professional Footballer, 1976, p. 45.

8 The beauty of football is its plasticity; each country that embraces it has something new to give; British efficiency and endurance, Latin flair and fire, South American virtuosity and acrobatics, Central European perfectionism.
Brian Glanville
The Footballer's Companion (ed.), 1962, p. 15.

9 My name is Jimmy Greaves. I am a professional footballer. And I am an alcoholic.
Jimmy Greaves
This One's On Me, 1979, cover.

10 Born on the streets, nurtured in the Public Schools and fathered by The Football Association, football owes its greatness and the rapid and sturdy growth of its youth to the principles of the Cup Competition.
Geoffrey Green
The Official History of the FA Cup, 1949, p. 9.

11 Football is easily understood by everybody, its rules are simple, it also has spectacular appeal. But along with its clarity, football remains mysterious, surprising and . . . not at all simple.
Gyula Grosics
Sport in the USSR, Oct., 1981, p. 27.

12 After whisky, footballers have been the favourite and most expensive export from Scotland to England.
Jimmy Guthrie
Soccer Rebel: The Evolution of the Professional Footballer, 1976, p. 14.

13 The growth of football is not a footnote in the social history of the twentieth century but a plain thread in it.
Arthur Hopcraft.
The Football Man, 1970, p. 22.

14 Improvisation is the hardest skill of all to counter.
Bob Hughes
The Sunday Times Magazine.

15 The coach means a lot but it's the players who play.
Kevin Keegan

Sport in the USSR, Apr., 1980, p. 36.

16 Soccer has three kinds of players;
Those who watch the ball
Those who watch the other players
Those who watch space.
The most limited players are those who watch the ball. The most advanced are those who look for and exploit available space.
A. E. Maher

Scholastic Coach, Aug., 1978.

17 Some monopolies may arise either through the possession of land containing particular minerals, spa water or a desirable location. Other monopolies may reflect freakish ability – Maria Callas's voice; George Best's feet.
B. J. McCormick et al
(Natural causes – one of the ways in which a Monopoly may arise.)

Introducing Economics, 1974, p. 334.

18 A man who had missed the last home match of 't'United had to enter social life on tiptoe in Bruddersford.
J. B. Priestley

The Good Companions.

Quoted by Anton Rippon.

Soccer: The Road to Crisis, 1983, p. 15.

19 To say that these men paid their shillings to watch twenty-two hirelings kick a ball is merely to say that a violin is wood and catgut, that *Hamlet* is so much paper and ink. For a shilling the Bruddersford United AFC offered you Conflict and Art.
J. B. Priestley

Ibid.

20 The principles of play are far more important than systems of play.
Mike Smith

Success in Football, 1982, p. 9.

21 Cinema and football alike can be understood as culturally-available opportunities of escape from work in the negative sense or, more positively, in the psychoanalytical sense for escape into fantasy.
Ian Taylor
'Football Mad: A Speculative Sociology of Football Hooliganism', in Eric Dunning (ed.), *The Sociology of Sport: A Selection of Readings*, 1971, p. 364.

22 Football is all very well as a game for rough girls, but is hardly suitable for delicate boys.
Oscar Wilde
(In conversation)
Quoted by Alvin Redman.
The Epigrams of Oscar Wilde, 1952.

FOOTBALL (AUSTRALIAN RULES)

1 Football is a great character builder. A lad learns to give and take hard knocks. He begins to understand the meaning of mateship.
Bruce Andrew
Foreword in Dick Wordley (ed.), *How to Play Aussie Rules*, 1963.

2 Kicking across goals is the type of thing that makes old men out of coaches.
Terry Callan
Ibid., p. 44.

3 If there comes a time when there is a real 'blue' then you have to be in it . . .
Bob Davis
Ibid., p. 3.

4 Ninety-nine per cent of Aussie Rules players are typical Australian citizens.
   Thorold Merrett

Ibid., p. 40.

5 Baulking is a much-vexed question.
   John Nicholls

Ibid., p. 62.

6 The disdain many intellectuals feel for the activities of the masses does not so often extend to football which secures often fanatical support from men one would not, from their pretensions in other areas, have suspected of harbouring a secret admiration for the game and the men who play it.
   Anne Summers
   Quoted by Stephen Murray-Smith.
   The Dictionary of Australian Quotations, 1984, p. 257.

7 You can sacrifice a lot of your own worth by using excess vigor.
   Roy Wright
   In Dick Wordley (ed.), *How to Play Aussie Rules*, 1963, p. 68.

GOLF

1 All games are silly, I suppose, but golf, if you look at it dispassionately, goes to extremes.
   Peter Alliss

Bedside Golf, 1980, p. 6.

2 Drive for show and putt for dough.
   Anonymous

3 Golf is a game where a man places a small sphere on top of a larger sphere and attempts to dislodge the small sphere from the larger sphere.
   Anonymous
   Quoted by Ted Ray.

Golf – My Slice of Life, 1972, p. 27.

Mens sana in corpore sano
A healthy mind in a healthy body.

157 – 9 — Raskins

4 The game of golf fulfils the axioms laid down for a perfect exercise – a walk with an object.
James Cantlie
Physical Efficiency, 1906, p. 204.

5 Funny game, golf, especially the way I play it.
Henry Cooper
Henry Cooper's Book of Boxing, 1982, p. 11.

6 No castles tower higher and more glittering in the air than golfing castles.
Bernard Darwin
'Know Your Weakness', in Peter Ryde (ed.),
Mostly Golf: A Bernard Darwin Anthology, 1976, p. 109.

7 When television first focused a Cyclopean eye on American professional golf the match play form of the game was turned to stone.
Peter Dobereiner
The Observer, Jan. 15, 1984, p. 42.

8 The best way to put is the way you put best.
Editors of *Golf Magazine*
Golf Magazine's Handbook of Putting, 1973, p. 32.

9 Putting with success is easy for some, difficult for others, and important to all, but it is never permanent for anyone.
Editors of *Golf Magazine*
Ibid., p. 138.

10 . . . if you can drive further with a putter than with a wood then by all means do so.
Michael Green
The Art of Coarse Golf, 1975, p. 44.

11 The number of shots taken by an opponent who is out of sight is equal to the square root of the sum of the number of curses heard plus the number of swishes.
Michael Green
Ibid., p. 83.

12 Bad putting is usually caused by evil spirits . . .
Michael Green
Ibid., p. 89.

13 If you watch a game, it's fun. If you play it, it's recreation. If you work at it, it's golf.
    Bob Hope

    Reader's Digest, Oct., 1958.
    Quoted by the *Home Book of Humorous Quotations*, 1967.

14 The hardest thing to learn about golf is keeping quiet about it.
    George Houghton

    Golfers in Orbit, 1968, p. 7.

15 You'd better be careful any time you play golf with President Johnson – he always brings his own Birdies.
    Vice President Hubert H. Humphrey
    (On President Johnson's golf game)

    'Scorecard', *Sports Illustrated*, Aug. 26, 1968, p. 11.

16 The devoted golfer is an anguished soul who has learned a lot about putting, just as an avalanche victim has learned a lot about snow.
    Dan Jenkins

    Sports Illustrated, Jul. 16, 1962, p.56.

17 As with so much in life which gives pleasure, perversity has decreed that most of the rules of golf and society are prohibitory in character.
    Don Lewis

    After-Dinner Golf, 1976, p. 13.

18 Golf is a fascinating game. It has taken me nearly forty years to discover that I can't play it!
    Ted Ray

    Golf – My Slice of Life, 1972, p. 13.

19 If a lot of people gripped a knife and fork like they do a golf club, they'd starve to death.
    Sam Snead

    'Scorecard', *Sports Illustrated*, Aug. 8, 1966, p. 12.

20 The only reason I ever played golf in the first place was so I could afford to hunt and fish.
    Sam Snead

    'Scorecard', *Sports Illustrated*, Jan. 22, 1968, p. 13.

21 A good golf swing is simply useless in any other human pursuit.
    Bernard Suits
    'The Elements of Sport', in R. G. Osterhoudt (ed.),
    The Philosophy of Sport: A Collection of
    Original Essays, 1973, p. 57.

22 I'm hitting the driver so good, I gotta dial the operator for long
    distance after I hit it.
    Lee Trevino
    'What They Are Saying', *The New York Times*, May 21, 1978.

23 I'm not saying my golf game went bad, but if I grew tomatoes
    they'd come up sliced.
    Lee Trevino
    'Coaches' Corner', *Scholastic Coach*, Dec., 1982, p. 38.

GREYHOUND RACING

1 A greyhound should be heeded lyke a snake,
    And neckyd lyke a drake,
    Backed lyke a bream,
    Footed lyke a catte,
    Taylled lyke a ratte.
    Dame Juliana Berners (1486)
    Quoted by John Arlott (ed.),
    The Oxford Companion to Sports and Games, 1975, p. 444.

2 I see you stand like greyhounds in the slips,
    William Shakespeare
    (King Henry), *The Life of King Henry the Fifth*,
    act III, sc. I, l. 31.

3 (*Slender*) How does your fallow greyhound, sir? I heard say he
    was outrun on Cotsall . . .
    (*Page*) A cur, sir.
    (*Shallow*) Sir he's a good dog, and a fair dog; can there be more
    said? He is good and fair.
    William Shakespeare
    The Merry Wives of Windsor, act I, sc. I, l. 92.

4   Edward and Richard, like a brace of greyhounds
    Having the fearful flying hare in sight,
    William Shakespeare
>   (Queen Margaret), *Third Part of King Henry the Sixth*,
>   act II, sc. V, l. 129.

GYMNASTICS

1   There are certain sports where physical perfection is transferred
    to a different level into art, the art of eurhythmic movement,
    an art related to ballet. Gymnastics is such a sport.
    Anonymous
>   *Sport in the USSR*, Sep., 1980, p. 39.

2   Gymnastics, when properly taught, can improve qualities of
    social fitness such as co-operation, conservation, tolerance,
    courtesy, leadership and fellowship, helpfulness, appreciation
    for the abilities of others, and fair play.
    James A. Baley
>   *Handbook of Gymnastics in the Schools*, 1974, p. 2.

3   Gymnastics, taught in a creative way, can ensure for every child
    the satisfaction of success. Since there are no set exercises
    with predetermined standards, the sense of failure is largely
    eliminated.
    Don Buckland
>   *Gymnastics: Activity in the Primary School*, 1978, p. 1.

4   Gymnastics is largely concerned with the management and
    transference of weight.
    DES (Department of Education and Science)
>   *Movement: Physical Education in the Primary Years*,
>   1972, part 1, p. 10.

5   Control and versatility in the use of the body are the essence
    of gymnastics
    DES
>   Ibid., part 2, p. 25.

6 Gymnastics includes movement on the floor and on apparatus; the two are complementary.
DES

Ibid., part 2, p. 38.

7 The Handstand is the gymnast's 'life line'.
Pauline Prestidge

Better Gymnastics, 1978, p. 31.

8 Beauty does not depend entirely on difficulty, but on rhythm, the ease and excellence of execution, graceful and elegant patterns – in short, style.
Jay Shaw

Scholastic Coach, Mar., 1981, p. 53.

9 Rhythm, harmony, fluency, form and composition are the essential qualities sought by the gymnast.
Jay Shaw

Ibid.

10 Rhythm is that which gives all work, all sport, all life its efficiency and delight, or to put it more fully, the intuitive understanding of the wave-movement between rest and effort, between run-up and throw, between confident relaxation and calm completion.
Torsten Tegnér
Quoted by Maja Carlquist.

Rhythmical Gymnastics: The book of the Sofia Girls, translated by R. E. Roper et al., 1955, p. 1.

HISTORY

1 For the professional historian, athletics has long been considered a subject beyond the scope, or perhaps better, beneath the contempt, of academic concern.
Anthony O. Edmonds

'The Second Louis-Schmeling Fight – Sport, Symbol and Culture', *Journal of Popular Culture*, vol. III, no. 1, Summer, 1973, p. 42.

2 Most games have their origin in the spare-time activities of a leisured class.
   H. A. Harris
   Sport in Britain: Its Origins and Development, 1975, p. 79.

3 It is my profound conviction that sport and physical education have been an active civilizing force in the twentieth century.
   Philip Noel-Baker
   'Sport and International Understanding', in E. Jokl and
   E. Simon (ed.), *International Research in Sport and Physical Education*, 1964, p. 3.

4 History and art have recorded sports in words and beauty; science and philosophy are tugged-at by its means and meanings; but the soul of sport remains uncaptured.
   Mary Pavlich Roby
   'The Power of Sport', in Ellen W. Gerber (ed.),
   Sport and the Body: A Philosophical Symposium, 1974,
   p. 215.

5 Although sports have played their part in history they have failed to make much impression upon historiography.
   James Walvin
   The People's Game: The Social History of British Football, 1975,
   p. 2.

HOCKEY
(FIELD)

1 Hockey is a reaching game.
   Mildred J. Barnes
   Field Hockey: The Coach and the Player, 1969, p. 197.

2 So many sporting activities have nowadays become businesses, but hockey is, and I hope always will be, a leisure-time entertainment.
   Vera Chapman
   Tackle Hockey This Way, 1961, intro.

3 Playing in goal is a battle of wits between you and the opposition
– it is most pleasing when you win, but rather noticeable when
you lose!
Rachael Heyhoe
> *'Just for Kicks': A Guide to Hockey Goalkeeping*, intro.

4 The greatest thing to be derived from playing hockey is
enjoyment.
Brenda Read
> *Better Hockey for Girls*, 1971, p. 96.

5 An umpire in Australia undoubtedly needs to be deaf – in both
ears.
Patrick Rowley
(On gamesmanship in Australian hockey)
> *World Hockey*, Dec., 1981, p. 13.

HOCKEY (ICE)

1 A hungry player is the best player, and the hungry coach is the
best coach.
Don Cherry
Quoted by Parton Keese.
> *The New York Times*, May 16, 1978.

2 When I was a coach at Rochester they called me in and said:
'We're making a change in your department.' I was the only
guy in my department.
Don Cherry
Quoted by Parton Keese.
> Ibid.

3 I went to a fight the other night and a hockey game broke out.
Rodney Dangerfield
> 'Scorecard', *Sports Illustrated*, Sep. 4, 1978, p. 16.

4 Canada is a country whose main exports are hockey players and
   cold fronts. Our main imports are baseball players and acid
   rain.
   Pierre Trudeau
   (Canadian Prime Minister)
   > 'Scorecard', *Sports Illustrated*, Jul. 26, 1982, p. 12.

HORSE RACING

1 Sport of Kings.
   Anonymous

2 To me a horse is like a bar of soap. Every time you wash your
   hands you take a little of the bar away. That's why I don't race
   my horses too much and never have.
   Melvin (Sunshine) Calvert
   > 'Scorecard', *Sports Illustrated*, Apr. 17, 1967, p. 20.

3 Racing is not a place where praise gushes. Tribute is a rivulet
   which only gathers force down the years.
   James Lawton
   > *Lester Piggott*, 1980, p. 8.

4 Racing, whatever else it inspires, certainly produces no
   indifference.
   Jack Leach
   > *A Rider on the Stand: Racing Reminiscences*, 1970, intro.

5 The professional horseman is a thorough individualist. He has
   to be, for his hand is against every man, and every man's hand
   is against him.
   Jack Leach
   > Ibid., p. 14.

6 Horses are like people – most of them are fairly normal.
   Jack Leach
   > Ibid., p. 93.

7 It was a nice change for some of us to be identified with a horse that applies the Garbo principle at the right end of the field.
Hugh McIlvanney
(On Slip Archer winning the Derby)
The Observer, Jun. 9, 1985.

8 You can teach a jockey many things, but there is something you cannot transmit. It is the feeling, the sensitivity of a natural jockey. It is a great mystery which only the horse, the great jockey, and God can really know about.
Noel Murless (Attributed)
Quoted by James Lawton.
Lester Piggott, 1980, p. 4.

9 There are, they say, fools, bloody fools, and men who remount in a steeplechase.
John Oaksey
Quoted by Jonathon Green.
A Dictionary of Contemporary Quotations, 1982, p. 344.

10 Horsemen recognize three categories of jockeys: 'honest-boys', 'money jocks' and 'businessmen'.
Marvin B. Scott
'The Man on the Horse',
in J. W. Loy Jr. and G. S. Kenyon (ed.),
Sport, Culture and Society, 1969, p. 431.

11 The Downs are very famous for horse-matches as there is not a properer place in the world for this sport.
James Toland (1711)
Quoted by David Hunn.
Epsom Racecourse: Its Story and its People, 1973.

12 Horse-racing I hate.
A. Trollope
'Australian Sports', in T. D. Jaques and G. R. Pavia (ed.),
Sport in Australia: Selected Readings in Physical Activity, p. 25.

13 Horses are like children, they'll learn something bad quicker than they'll learn something good . . .
Philip Walsh
Stable Rat: Life in the Racing Stables, 1979, p. 72.

HUMOUR

1 He has the gift, unusual among top sportsmen, for the bon mot, and his delivery is that of an ace comedian.
John Ballantine
(On Lee Trevino)

The Times, Jul. 8, 1970.

2 Every runner has at least one dog story.
James F. Fixx
The Complete Book of Running, 1979, p. 145.

3 I have no interest in sailing round the World. Not that there is any lack of requests for me to do so.
Edward Heath
The Observer, Jun. 19, 1977.

4 One day of practice is like one day of clean living. It doesn't do you any good.
Abe Lemon
'Coaches' Corner', *Scholastic Coach*, Apr., 1979.

ICE SKATING

1 Skating I never really cared very much for, except as it gave an excellent opportunity for making love to girls.
Gamaliel Bradford
(Oct. 15, 1916)
The Journal of Gamaliel Bradford 1883–1932 (ed.),
Van Wyck Books, 1933.

2 Skating is always bracing and exhilarating; to some the rapidity of the motion through the keen frosty air which it affords is almost ecstatic.
Frederick W. Hackwood
Old English Sports, 1907, p. 23.

3 A figure skater, even a champion, is no better than his mastery
of the primary edges.
Maribel Vinson Owen

> *The Fun of Figure Skating*, 1960, intro.

4 There is one rule that seems to apply to every one of us who
takes up the 'art sport' in all its many aspects: Once a skater,
always a skater.
Maribel Vinson Owen

> Ibid., p. 167.

5 . . . then over the parke (where I first in my life, it being a
great frost, did see people sliding with their sckeates, which is
a very pretty art) . . .
Samuel Pepys

> *The Diary of Samuel Pepys*, Dec. 1, 1662.

JOURNALISM/ TELEVISION

1 Sport is one of the great factors in the lives of tens of thousands
of Britishers, and yet there are supercilious gentlemen who
speak and write of sport as though it were just the merest side
issue.
Eugene Corri

> *Thirty Years a Boxing Referee*, 1915, p. 233.

2 Television has done to sport, in a sense, what film has to drama:
transformed it into a new electronic medium.
Ron Cummings
'Double Play and Replay: Living out there is Television Land',
> *Journal of Popular Culture*, 1974/5, p. 426.

3   Sport and art offer us the possibility as participants of creative
self-expression, a means of fulfilment and completion, a sense
of identity, and of social recognition. But most of us remain
outside the inside story as vicarious spectators. That glass across
the tube is a real barrier.
Ron Cummings

Ibid., p. 432.

4   Writing about sport is worth nothing without gusto.
Bernard Darwin
Quoted by Peter Ryde.
Mostly Golf: A Bernard Darwin Anthology, 1976.

5   Bernard Darwin and Neville Cardus took the shine off the ball
in the battle against penny-a-line journalese and then Longhurst
came along to win the match.
Peter Dobereiner
The Observer, Jul. 23, 1978.

6   When you talk about the link between television and sport,
you start thinking in terms of millions of dollars, because that
is what the link is all about. Millions of dollars.
Paul Gardner
Nice Guys Finish Last: Sport and American Life, 1974, p. 32.

7   Those of us who devotedly read the sports pages of newspapers
know very well that the language of sports reporting is full of
clichés, effete adjectives and the kind of instant appraisal which
is meant to demonstrate the reporter's profound knowledge of
the game.
Zulfikar Ghose
'The Language of Sports Reporting', in H. T. A. Whiting and
D. W. Masterson (ed.), *Readings in the Aesthetics of Sport*,
1974, p. 57.

8   Give the clever editors a run, and they will turn a football match
into something which has nothing much to do with football, but
is often a splendid spectacle in itself. Show the whole thing
live, and the dreadful inadequacies of the parasitic medium
become blatantly clear. No panoramic view. No atmosphere.
Brian Glanville
(On the live transmission of Football matches)
The Sunday Times, Jan. 15, 1983.

9 A sports commentator should, above all else, be keen. Keen on sport. Even more precisely, he should love it.
E. Grafov
Sport in the USSR, Jan., 1981, p. 42

10 For better or worse, sport in the second half of the twentieth century has capitulated to the commercial speculator; a process accelerated by the international scope of television as a purveyor of instant play, inter-play, and re-play.
Doug Ibbotson
Sporting Scenes, 1980, p. 137.

11 All sports are achingly vulnerable to reductio ad absurdum. Which leads us straight to television.
James Kaplan
'How TV changes Sports', in *Dial*, Jul., 1982, p. 46.

12 California shared the Olympics with the athletes of the world, I suppose, but first and foremost it shared them with ABC TV.
Frank Keating
The Guardian, Aug. 14, 1984, p. 21.

13 Not in literature or in music must we seek the image of sport, but in the press, in photography and television.
René Maheu
'Cultural Anthropology', in E. Jokl and E. Simon (ed.), *International Research in Sport and Physical Education*, 1964, p. 19.

14 The capacity of sporting journalists to wax lyrical in face of the exceptional is only matched by the speed with which they run out of adjectives in doing so.
Derek Malcolm
Quoted by Dorian Williams.
The Horseman's Companion, 1967, p. 248.

15 Nobility is no more frequently witnessed by sports writers than by anybody else and the least we can do is acknowledge it when we see it.
Hugh McIlvanney
(Writing about Eusebio Pedrozo)
The Observer, Jun. 16, 1985, p. 39.

16 Not only do they know nothing about football, but if you were to shut them up in a room by themselves, they couldn't even write a letter to mother.
Cesar Menotti
(On his country's journalists)
'Inside Track', *The Sunday Times*, Aug. 22, 1982.

17 Television turns players into people and uniform numbers into personalities.
Steve Miller
'Television and Sports: The Ties That Bind',
USA Today, Nov., 1984, p. 81.

18 Give television enough time and it'll rid the world of good taste.
Zander Pepe
'Coaches' Corner', *Scholastic Coach*, Sep., 1980, p. 80.

19 I always turn to the sports section first. The sports page records people's accomplishments; the front page has nothing but man's failures.
Earl Warren
(Chief Justice of the USA)
'Scorecard', *Sports Illustrated*, Jul. 22, 1968, p. 11.

JUDO/KARATE

1 (Judo) It is an art, a science, a philosophy, even a way of life.
E. G. Bartlett
Basic Judo, 1974, p. 7.

2 Judo style and skill is largely a reflection or projection of the fighter's personality.
Geof Gleeson
All about Judo, 1975, p. 68.

3 Judo is a very fragile plant, it has had something of a hypochondriachal existence.
Geof Gleeson

Ibid., p. 137.

4 Judo, like so many truly indigenous sports, is a microcosm of its enveloping society, a reflection of national habits and customs.
G. R. Gleeson

Anatomy of Judo, 1969, p. 19.

5 Judo is not only an ideal system of self-defence; it is indeed an art the sedulous practice of which is almost certain to render its votaries physically fit.
E. J. Harrison

Judo for Beginners, 1958, p. 8.

6 Judo may be epitomized as the art of destroying your opponent's balance; unless and until you have done this you cannot hope to defeat him.
E. J. Harrison

Ibid.

7 Karate is a system of unarmed combat, practised as a highly competitive sport.
C. J. Mack

Karate Test Techniques: The Main Contest Techniques for Beginner and Black Belt, 1971, p. 15.

LAW

1 A sport is, at base, nothing but a set of rules and if they are too flagrantly flouted the sport that is built on them collapses.
Paul Gardner

Nice Guys Finish Last: Sport and American Life, 1974, p. 61.

2 The playing area creates the greatest scope for errors, ignorance
and misunderstanding relating sport to law and law to sport.
Edward Grayson
Sport and the Law, 1978, p. 31.

3 Elastic bands are made to be stretched; laws, in my submission
are not.
J. Markson
Tennis Magazine, no. 38, Jan./Feb., 1984, p. 24.

4 In sports, law was born and also liberty, and the nexus of their
interrelation.
Michael Novak
The Joys of Sports, 1976, part 1, p. 43.

5 Laws may come and Laws may go, but the game goes on for
ever.
Admiral Sir Percy Royds
The History of the Laws of Rugby Football, 1949, p. ii.

LAWN TENNIS/ REAL TENNIS

1 Concentration is one of the most important things in lawn tennis
and without it even the best players cannot win.
Evelyn Dewhurst
Lawn Tennis Guaranteed (1939), 1950, p. 189.

2 I arrived late, in the orthodox costume – that is to say, a straw
hat which is oftener off than on, a flannel shirt two sizes too
large for me, and a pair of flannels . . .
F. B. Doveton
(At a Lawn Tennis Party)
A Fisherman's Fancies, 1895, p. 75.

3   When Ille Nastase plays John McEnroe, it's the only time the crowd calls for silence.
Jerry Girard
　　'Coaches' Corner', *Scholastic Coach*, Dec., 1979, p. 79.

4   Yumpies – young unfit municipal park players . . .
Simon Inglis
　　　　　　　　　　The Guardian, Jun. 20, 1985, p. 25.

5   All great players succeed because they master the principles of taking each movement as it comes and resist the temptation to panic and rush their shots.
C. M. Jones
　　　　　Tennis Magazine, no. 38, Jan./Feb., 1984, p. 16.

6   Ooh I say!
Dan Maskell
(Tennis commentator)

7   Between receiving coaching and playing in a real game there is a vacuum which, if a player wishes to reach a reasonably high standard, he or she must fill by dint of hard practice.
Jack Moore
　　　　　Action: British Journal of Physical Education,
　　　　　　　　　　vol. 12, no. 4, Jul., 1982, p. 103.

8   Every tennis 'doctor' at some time or another will be called upon to treat a case of virulent foot-faulting.
Fred A. Mulhauser
　　　　　Scholastic Coach, May/June., 1980, p. 46.

9   To the Tennis Court, and there saw the King play at tennis and others; but to see how the King's play was extolled, without any cause at all, was a loathsome sight . . .
Samuel Pepys
　　　　　The Diary of Samuel Pepys, Jan. 4, 1664.

10   There falling out at tennis;
William Shakespeare
　　(Polonius), *Hamlet, Prince of Denmark*, act II, sc. I, l. 59.

11   The faith they have in tennis and tall stockings.
William Shakespeare
　　　　(Sir Thomas Lovell), *The Famous History of the Life of
　　　　King Henry the Eighth*, act I, sc. III, l. 30.

12 When we have match'd our rackets to these balls,
    We will in France, by God's grace, play a set.
    William Shakespeare
            (King Henry the Fifth), *The Life of King Henry the Fifth*,
                                            act I, sc. II, l. 261.

13 In a sport where 'love' means nothing, it's not surprising that
    etiquette means everything.
    Molly Tyson
                                The New York Times, May 15, 1978.

LIFE SAVING

1 A person drowns if he allows the water to win.
   Michael Bettsworth
      A Technique for Water Survival: Drownproofing, 1976, p. 8.

2 Swimming should be fun but it should not be dangerous fun.
   Margaret Jarvis
                Survival Swimming and Life Saving, 1976, p. 11.

3 The essence of 'good' life saving is the effective use of
   initiative . . .
   Clive Patrickson
                Action: British Journal of Physical Education,
                        vol. II, no. 5, Sept., 1980, p. 121.

4 QUEMCUNQUE MISERUM VIDERIS HOMINEM SCIAS
   (whomsoever you see in distress, recognise in him a fellow man)
   The Royal Life Saving Society
                Life Saving and Water Safety, 1982, p. 8.

MODERN PENTATHLON

1 One of the great values of the modern pentathlon, with its challenge of five different competitions, is the manner in which it fosters the spirit of independence.
Frigyes Hegedüs
Modern Pentathlon, 1968, p. 16.

2 Training in modern pentathlon is like a rehearsal on a stopped revolving stage leaving the actors to do the turns themselves.
Frigyes Hegedüs
Ibid., p. 78.

3 Modern pentathlon is half-way between the sports that can be measured by absolute standards and those where the standards are relative.
Frigyes Hegedüs
Ibid., p. 235.

MONEY/ SPONSORSHIP

1 As soon as a sport becomes a business, it becomes subject to the laws of the marketplace, the equations of supply and demand that control any commercial operation. A profit has to be made. Tickets have to be sold and sponsors found. Nothing sells tickets or attracts sponsors like winning. And so it becomes a case of win or bust.
Andrew Bailey
Future Sport, 1982, p. 26.

2 There is no business like show business – except sports business.
William J. Baker
Sports in the Western World, 1982, p. 304.

3 As the economic dog wags the tail of sports, much of modern sport seems twisted and bent out of shape.
William J. Baker
Ibid., p. 330.

4 Getting an athlete to sign a contract can be an expensive venture. But getting him to sign anything else – a photograph, a baseball, a personal letter or just a scrap of paper – can be like getting him to write you a check.
Jim Benagh
The New York Times, Jul. 7, 1980, p. C2.

5 Clearly sport rests on an economic foundation.
Harry Edwards
Sociology of Sport, 1973, p. 273.

6 When money enters into sport corruption is sure to follow.
E. N. Gardiner
Athletics of the Ancient World, 1930, p. 103.

7 They can talk about black power and white power. I believe in green power: money, man, money.
Reggie Harding
'Scorecard', *Sports Illustrated*, Oct. 8, 1966, p. 21.

8 Over the last decade, money has done more than make the Sports World go round. It has made it spin off its axis.
Gary Pomerantz
Washington Post, Jul. 10, 1983.

9 There is money in sport.
George H. Sage
Sport and American Society: Selected Readings, 1970, p. 154.

10 The sponsorship of sport provides a service to the whole of sport and to the community which sport serves; in this respect therefore it also serves the public interest.
The Central Council of Physical Recreation
Committee of Enquiry into Sports Sponsorship,
The Howell Report, 1983, conclusion 1, 1.1.

11 Sport is no longer simply concerned with physical recreation
and joy in skill, grace, and sheer activity. It is 'big business'.
Richard Thompson

Race and Sport, 1964, p. 1.

MOTOR CYCLE RACING

1 A contending motocrosser can expect to play out sooner than
a fighter or football player. There is no retirement plan.
Thomas McGuane

An Outside Chance: Essays on Sport, 1980, p. 36.

2 Motocross is very properly considered a sport. It requires
strength, the balance of a slack-wire walker, incredible coordination, and endurance. . . . The paunches and bubble buts of
other motor sports are not seen here.
Thomas McGuane

Ibid.

3 It is a duellist's game.
Thomas McGuane
(On motocross)

Ibid., p. 42.

4 Most sports have a masonic element in which the technical
terms act as passwords, . . . in motorcycling this element is
overwhelming.
Geoffrey Nicholson

The Professionals, 1964, p. 165.

5 Unless you're fond of hollering you don't make great conver-
sations on a running cycle.
Robert M. Pirsig
Zen and the Art of Motor Cycle Maintenance, 1974, part 1,
p. 7.

6 That's all the motorcycle is, a system of concepts worked out in steel.
Robert M. Pirsig

Ibid., p. 94.

7 Unlike many other popular spectator and participant sports, it allows the emphasis upon entertainment to equal that laid upon the final result.
Martin Rogers
(On speedway)

The Illustrated History of Speedway, 1978, p. 8.

MOTOR RACING

1 Grand Prix motor racing is like *Punch*. It is never as good as it was.
Maxwell Boyd

The Observer Magazine, Sep. 25, 1983.

2 Lady Docker was to post-war motoring as Salvador Dali was to between-war painting: she outraged and, at the same time, delighted.
Richard Garrett

Motoring and the Mighty, 1971, p. 181.

3 Motor racing has had more than its share of legends; more than its fill of tragedy.
Barrie Gill

Motor Racing: The Grand Prix Greats, 1972.

4 You appreciate that it is very easy to die and you have to arrange your life to cope with that reality.
Niki Lauda

The Observer, Oct. 3, 1982.

5 It is necessary to relax your muscles when you can. Relaxing your brain is fatal.
Stirling Moss

> *Newsweek*, May 16, 1955,
> Quoted by *The Home Book of Humorous Quotations*, 1967.

6 When the first 'horseless carriage' was timed for acceleration, drag racing began.
David J. Neuman

> 'A Social Perspective of Drag Racing',
> *Journal of Popular Culture*, 1974/5, p. 169.

7 We did it for Britain and for the hell of it.
Richard Noble
(On breaking the world land-speed record)

> 'The Week in Words', *The Sunday Times*, Oct. 9, 1983.

8 Italians are distinguished by their disrespect for speed limits and preference for flair over civil obedience.
Jackie Stewart

> *Jackie Stewart on the Road*, 1983, p. 14.

9 The World landspeed record requires the minimum of skill, and the maximum of courage.
Tommy Wisdom
Quoted by Phil Drackett.

> *The Story of Malcolm and Donald Campbell*, 1969, p. 7.

MOVEMENT/DANCE

1 The teacher, engaged in observing, placating, stimulating, and encouraging children, excited or depressed, happy or sad, is a person who cannot fail to be aware of the rhythmic qualities which underlie human existence.
V. R. Bruce

> *Movement in Silence and Sound*, 1970, p. 1.

2 We live in an environment of rhythm.
   V. R. Bruce

                                                              Ibid.

3 Common to all aspects of physical education is movement.
   Barbara Churcher
                      Physical Education for Teaching, 1971, p. 22.

4 Dancing is an instinctive inclination, an inborn rhythmic
   urge . . .
   Claudette Collins
                      Practical Modern Educational Dance, 1969, p. 1.

5 The Modern Dance is not a thing . . . it is a structural event.
   Louis Danz
    In Merle Armitage (ed.), *Martha Graham* (1937), 1963, p. 78.

6 The elements of dance are space, time and human bodies.
   Agnes De Mille
                              The Book of the Dance, 1963, p. 7.

7 Dancing employs rhythm in both spheres – audible and visual.
   It is a time-space art, and the only one.
   Agnes De Mille

                                                        Ibid., p. 8.

8 Sports require skill, coordination and strength, but they are
   not dancing nor the stuff of dancing. Even when pleasing to
   watch, their real meaning lies in the practical results: the food
   caught, the game won, the record set.
   Agnes De Mille

                                                        Ibid., p. 9.

9 Dancing moves us. It excites us. It compels or persuades us.
   Agnes De Mille

                                                       Ibid., p. 13.

10 Dance consists of three types of movement: instinctive actions
   and expressions, sign language, and dance steps.
   Agnes De Mille

                                                       Ibid., p. 18.

11 The art of the dancer and the record of the athlete represent man's supreme achievements in movement.
DES (Department of Education and Science)
> *Movement: Physical Education in the Primary Years,*
> 1972, part 1, p. 3.

12 Movement experiences of all kinds are of interest to the physical educationist, since facility or understanding of movement in one context is likely to have relevance in another.
DES
> Ibid., part 1, p. 8.

13 Movement provides a two-way channel of learning, being both a way of finding out and a form of accomplishment.
DES
> Ibid.

14 Physical education, using movement as its medium of learning and expression, is an integral part of the education process.
DES
> Ibid.

15 Movement, as the language of dance, has the whole body as the instrument of expression.
DES
> Ibid., part 2, p. 45.

16 Rhythm . . . is common and divine.
Ann Driver
> *Music and Movement,* 1936, p. 3.

17 To each his own rhythm is a natural law.
Ann Driver
> Ibid., p. 6.

18 The child must learn the levels of space around his own body just as he must learn the seven notes of the musical scale, and the primary and complementary colours of his paint-box.
Ann Driver
> Ibid., p. 20.

19 That boys need any power of expression in movement other than that which is competitive and athletic is unfortunately somewhat of a revolutionary idea to-day.
Ann Driver

Ibid., p. 61.

20 Man has always danced and always will.
Grace Fielder
The Rhythmic Program for Elementary Schools, 1952, p. 18.

21 Athletes, gymnasts and high divers know, exactly, in terms of skill, what they are about; but the more they specialise, and specialise they must, the narrower their practice becomes, and what they know of themselves in terms of their medium – movement – is similarly restricted.
Ruth Foster
Knowing in my Bones, 1976, p. 10.

22 In all its ramifications dance can be defined as rhythmic human movement performed as an outlet for or an expression of ideas or emotions.
A. H. Franks
Social Dance: A Short History, 1963, p. 1.

23 Movement . . . is the most ephemeral of all human activities.
A. H. Franks

Ibid., p. 26.

24 Dance need not change . . . it has only to stand revealed.
Martha Graham
In Merle Armitage (ed.), *Martha Graham* (1937), 1963, p. 88.

25 Movement in the modern dance is the product not of invention but of discovery . . . discovery of what the body will do, and what it can do in the expression of emotion.
Martha Graham

Ibid., p. 104.

26 Ballet is a modern art, dancing is prehistoric.
Arnold Haskell

Ballet, 1938, p. 17.

27   Ballet as we know it was born when the acrobatics of the professional and the aristocratic grace of the courtier were united.
Arnold Haskell

Ibid., p. 20.

28   The difference between dancing and acrobatics lies not so much in technique as in a state of mind.
Arnold Haskell

Ibid., p. 45.

29   Dance is an art performed by individuals or groups of human beings, existing in time and space, in which the human body is the instrument and movement in the medium.
Richard Kraus
   History of the Dance: In Art and Education, 1969, p. 13.

30   Movement is, so to speak, living architecture – living in the sense of changing emplacements as well as changing cohesion.
Rudolf Laban
         In L. Ullman (ed.), *Choreutics*, 1966, p. 5.

31   The feel of movement, the joy of the sensation of moving, is best experienced through repetition.
Peter Lofthouse

Dance, 1973, p. 11.

32   Dance is a significant activity in education because it gives form to feeling.
David McKittrick

Dance, 1972, p. 22.

33   Every artist walks a tightrope between intention and achievement.
John Percival
         Experimental Dance, 1971, part 2, p. 39.

34   If one thing is clear about the experiments being made in dance all over the world today, it is that nothing is clear.
John Percival

Ibid., p. 150.

35   Movement is one of the first means of expression, of communi-
cation and of learning about the world.
Joan Russell
Creative Dance: In The Primary School, 1975, p. 3.

36   It is because movement can be seen as the fundamental revel-
ation and expression of individual personality that one can see
dance, the art of movement, as a primary art.
Joan Russell
Creative Dance: In The Secondary School, 1969, p. 17.

37   Dance is the art which in the fullest measure expresses man's
rhythmical nature.
Joan Russell
Ibid., p. 18.

38   Music and Physical Education are on common ground wherever
music and movement take place simultaneously.
R. M. Thackray
Music and Physical Education, 1965, p. 3.

39   Movement education is that phase of the total education
programe which has as its contribution the development of
effective, efficient, and expressive movement responses in a
thinking, feeling, and sharing human being.
Joan Tillotson
'A Brief Theory of Movement Education', in R. T. Sweet (ed.),
Selected Readings in Movement Education, 1970, p. 33.

40   The medium of creativity granted me was the dance, always
and ever the dance.
Mary Wigman
The Language of Dance, translated by Walter Surell, 1966,
p. 8.

41   Time, strength, and space; these are the elements which give
the dance its life.
Mary Wigman
Ibid., p. 11.

42   Tennyson observed that of all things sculpture is one of the
most difficult to describe. Dancing is even more so.
Stark Young
In Merle Armitage (ed.), *Martha Graham* (1937), 1963, p. 49.

NATIONALITY

1 Whether we view sports as a reflection of the mores of American life or as the promoter of those mores, it is a sobering analysis to consider that they may represent the end result of American pragmatism.
   Arnold Beisser
                          The Madness in Sport, 1977, p. 146.

2 In short, E. Germany cultivates a sporting conception of the state and a state conception of sport.
   Jean-Marie Brohm
                 Sport – A Prison of Measured Time, 1978, p. 86.

3 Though nobody in the modern world holds a monopoly on sports frenzy, the Big Game happens only in America.
   E. H. Cady
   The Big Game: College Sports and American Life, 1978, p. 3.

4 Australia leads the world in the degree to which its sports interests and sports organizations reflect the total social and political ideals of the nation.
   R. Denney
   'The Spectatorial Forms', in J. W. Loy Jr. and G. S. Kenyon (ed.), *Sport, Culture and Society*, 1969, p. 340.

5 We English folks come of a very sporting family.
   P. H. Ditchfield
   Old English Sports: Pastimes and Customs (1891), 1975, p. 14.

6 Sport is the ultimate Australian super-religion, the one thing every Australian believes in passionately.
   K. Dunstan
                 'Our Sporting Obsession', in T. D. Jaques and
   G. R. Pavia (ed.), *Sport in Australia: Selected Readings in Physical Activity*, 1973, p. 2.

7 It seems to be a characteristic of the British to take a perfectly ordinary, even juvenile amusement and convert it into a highly organized, competitive sport or recreation.
   H.R.H. The Duke of Edinburgh
   Foreword in Michael Seth-Smith, *The Cresta Run*, 1976.

8 Obviously Australia is a country which takes its sport seriously.
   Otherwise she would hardly have enshrined the heart of a
   racehorse in her national capital, and parked the hide of the
   same lovely beast in a famous museum.
   H. Gordon

   'The Reasons Why', in T. D. Jaques
   and G. R. Pavia (ed.), *Sport in Australia: Selected Readings
   in Physical Activity*, 1973, p. 94.

9 The sports of the people afford an index to the character of the
   nation.
   Frederick W. Hackwood

   Old English Sports, 1907, p. 1.

10 Australian national heroes are largely cricketers, tennis-players,
   swimmers and boxers or even race-horses. Probably only Ned
   Kelly and the largely nameless heroes of ANZAC rival in the
   public imagination those who have gained fame in the sports
   arena or on the race-track.
   Dr W. Mandle

   'Cricket and Australian Nationalism in the Nineteenth
   Century', in T. D. Jaques and G. R. Pavia (ed.),
   Sport in Australia: Selected Readings in Physical Activity,
   1973, p. 46.

11 Australians are a race of 'sports'.
   Michael McKernan
   Quoted by Richard Cashman and Michael McKernan.
   Sport in History: The Making of Modern Sporting History, 1979,
   p. 1.

12 Americans are sportophiles.
   Steve Miller

   USA Today, Nov., 1984, p. 81.

NETBALL

1 I didn't like netball . . . I used to get wolf whistles because of
   my short skirts.
   H.R.H. Princess Anne
   　　　　'Sayings of the Week', *The Observer*, Sep. 18, 1983.

2 One distinctive feature of netball which should determine much
   of the tactical thinking . . . is that playing areas are severely
   restricted, and these restrictions, unlike those imposed in other
   games, are specific to each player.
   Sally Dewhurst-Hands
   　　　　　　Netball: A Tactical Approach, 1980, p. 16.

3 To abandon the teaching of netball to older girls is as sterile as
   neglecting academic study after the onset of puberty.
   Rita Lacey
   　　　　　　British Journal of Physical Education,
   　　　　　　　　vol. 10, no. 2, Mar., 1979, p. 44.

4 Netball is a game that requires a ball, a court, two rings and
   fourteen women. It requires leaps, lunges, outstretched hands
   and three-second decisions. Out of that comes one hour of
   amazing activity, a few whistle blasts and a lot of enjoyment.
   Toy Martin
   　　　　　　Netball Fundamentals, 1977, p. 5.

5 Netball is essentially a team game – a player's contribution
   must therefore be co-operation in every sense.
   Rena B. Stratford
   　　　　　　Netball, 1963, p. 119.

ORIENTEERING

1 The thought sport.
Anonymous
(Definition of Orienteering)
Quoted by Roger Smith.
The Penguin Book of Orienteering, 1982.

2 Cunning Running.
Anonymous
(Definition of Orienteering)
Quoted by Roger Smith.

Ibid.

3 Orienteering with its juxtaposition of mental awareness and
athletic fitness provides the ideal recreation for all those who
prefer the muscular mill to be oiled by skill and technical
ability.
John Disley
Orienteering, 1978, p. 16.

4 This is the complete sport, the body is exercised and the mind is
absorbed – the criterion of success is your personal enjoyment.
John Disley

Ibid., p. 162.

5 The sport of orienteering has all the significance of an
adventure.
Baron Gösta 'Rak' Lagerfelt
Foreword in Gordon Pirie, *The Challenge of Orienteering*,
1968, p. 9.

6 Orienteering is a mixture of geography, map-reading, mathe-
matics, intellect and character-training as well as physical
education.
Gordon Pirie
The Challenge of Orienteering, 1968, p. 22.

7 Orienteering is a 'Sport for All' in which the family wayfinder
   is just as important as the elite competitor.
   Brian Porteous
                                    Orienteering, 1978, p. 12.

8 On being faced with the word 'orienteering', people's reactions
   vary from thinking it's some new form of martial art from the
   East, through 'Oh yes, we did that in the Army (or scouts)' to
   blank incomprehension.
   Roger Smith
                     The Spur Book of Orienteering, 1979, p. 9.

PARACHUTING

1 Parachuting is a highly individualistic sport and needs individualistic training.
   Anonymous

2 'Relative work' is extremely dangerous in the case of incapable,
   imprudent and insensible men.
   Anonymous

3 I suffer from acrophobia. I can't look out of high buildings. I
   don't even like to ride in planes. When I'm in one, I want to
   jump out. I guess that's what makes me a good sky diver.
   Jeanni McCombs
           'Scorecard', *Sports Illustrated*, Jul. 25, 1966, p. 9.

4 If ever there was a sport that requires self-confidence and
   independence, parachuting is that sport.
   Bud Sellick
                *Parachutes and Parachuting: A Modern Guide
                           to the Sport*, 1971, p. 153.

5 In freefall the body can do everything an aeroplane can do
   except go back up!
   Sally Smith
                       Parachuting and Skydiving, 1978, p. 10.

PHILOSOPHY

1 World sport is an integral part of world culture; its forms can serve to develop aesthetic taste and can satisfy the need for artistic expression.
Don Anthony
A Strategy for British Sport, 1980, p. 5.

2 From running I derive not just physical but aesthetic pleasure.
Filbert Bayi
Sport in the USSR, Jan., 1981, p. 17.

3 . . . great sport has intellectual beauty.
R. Carlisle
'Physical Education and Aesthetics', in H. T. A. Whiting and D. W. Masterson (ed.), *Readings in the Aesthetics of Sport*, 1974, p. 26.

4 The goddess of sport is not Beauty but Victory, a jealous goddess who demands an absolute homage.
R. K. Elliott
'Aesthetics in Sport', Ibid., p. 111.

5 Each teacher, coach, athlete who has been extensively involved in sport knows that it touches on his or her own sense of being-in-the-world.
E. W. Gerber
Sport and the Body: A Philosophical Symposium (ed.), 1974, p. 67.

6 Perhaps more fundamental than either the perceptual or ideational reality of sport, is its metaphysical existence as an experience.
E. W. Gerber
Ibid., p. 69.

7 Whether he is hurling a javelin, soaring off a ski-jump, performing a double back flip off a diving board, or screaming towards earth in a free fall sky dive, man is alone. He is beyond the world of public determinations; of official identities; of func-

tions; of self-deceptions and of everydayness. And in the solitary
state of oneness, man can meet himself.
William A. Harper

'Man Alone', Ibid., p. 101.

8 The beauty of human motion as a dialectical unit of technique
and style thus becomes one of the basic assumptions of the self-
realisation of man.
V. Hohler

'The Beauty of Motion', in H. T. A. Whiting and
D. W. Masterson (ed.), *Readings in the Aesthetics of Sport*,
1974, p. 49.

9 If one accepts the idea that happiness is measured by the
number of points at which a man touches life – the extent of
his continuing experience – then the knowledge that one can
perform athletic actions skilfully and in certain circles better
than most other people must increase one's total happiness.
L. A. Liversedge

'Medical Aspects of Sport and Physical Fitness',
paper presented at Manchester Statistical Society,
Dec. 11, 1963, p. 10.

10 Even the most prosaic of persons, whether participant or
observer, must at times encounter the feeling that human
movement, in addition to any functional justification has inde-
pendent value on the ground of beauty.
R. E. Morgan

Concerns and Values in Physical Education, 1974, ch. 4.

11 Rhythm is an aesthetic value perceived in variations of sequen-
tial emphasis.
R. E. Morgan

Ibid.

12 Sometimes there is an element of art in sport and scope for the
artist in the sportsman, though it is a limited one.
Louis Arnaud Reid

'Aesthetics and Education', in H. T. A. Whiting and
D. W. Masterson (ed.), *Readings in the Aesthetics of Sport*,
1974, p. 19.

13 The Athletic aesthetic is a tricky thing.
Michael Roberts

The New York Times, Mar. 6, 1977.

14 People outside of sport may only see the game, just as those outside of war only see the horror. Yet, in that horror a man may be better than he will ever be the rest of his life. And in that game a man may find what life is really all about.
George Sheehan
Dr Sheehan on Running, 1978, p. 189.

15 The understanding of being is clarified by sport.
H. Slusher
Man: Sport and Existence: A Critical Analysis, 1967, p. 5.

16 Peacefulness is everywhere, if we make it so; we need not go to the hills to seek it.
F. S. Smythe
The Valley of Flowers, 1938, p. 284.

17 In Soviet society, where work alone is the measure of a person's worth, sport is viewed as another opportunity given to a person to come to know himself, improve himself, fortify his health and form his character.
N. Terekhov
Sport in the USSR, Jan., 1983, p. 3.

PHYSICAL EDUCATION

1 Between play, sport and physical education there is overlap – and sometimes conflict.
Don Anthony
A Strategy for British Sport, 1980, p. 2.

2 Physical education can be defined as that integral part of the educational process which enhances and harmonises the physical, intellectual, social and emotional aspects of an individual's personality chiefly through directed physical activity.
P. J. Arnold
Education: Physical Education and Personality Development, 1972, p. 1.

3 Physical education is for the sake of mental and moral culture and not an end in itself. It is to make the intellect, feelings, and will more vigorous, sane, supple and resourceful.
G. Stanley Hall
Quoted by J. F. Williams.
The Principles of Physical Education (1927), 1964, p. 318.

4 A fundamental problem facing today's physical education teacher is how to handle the skill versus available time paradox, created by a highly expanded curriculum.
Lew Hardy
British Journal of Physical Education,
vol. 9, no. 6, Nov., 1978, p. 163.

5 It is unlikely that wheelchair sport will assume greater importance than non-disabled sport but a humanistic society should at least entertain the idea.
Chris A. Hopper
Action: British Journal of Physical Education,
vol. 14, no. 1, Jan/Feb., 1983, p. 7.

6 As yet we have no physical education which sends the whole body into action in company with the mind, the intelligence and the imagination.
Dr L. P. Jacks
Quoted by Ann Driver.
Music and Movement, 1936, p. 5.

7 The primary goal of physical education should be for each student to be well skilled in several different lifetime, leisure-oriented sport skills.
Dean A. Pease
'Physical Education: Accountability for the Future',
in Raymond Walsh (ed.), *Physical Education:
A view toward the future*, 1977, p. 145.

8 For the sake of analytical expediency, it may be convenient to talk of the human mind, the human body, or the human soul, but it is the human being who is the concern of education, and that beingis always whole.
Celeste Ulrich
'The Future Hour: An Educational View', Ibid., p. 124.

9   Physical education is concerned with the art and science of human movement. However, its ultimate objective is to employ movement in order to contribute to the physical, mental and social goals of education.
Carl E. Willgoose
> *The Curriculum in Physical Education*, 1979, p. 39.

10   Physical education bears an ancient heritage. Its sources rise out of the nature of man, its variations reflect the changing economic, industrial, religious and cultural environments of all people, and its purposes demonstrate the dominant ideals of the time and the place.
Jesse Feiring Williams
> *The Principles of Physical Education* (1927), 1964, p. 3.

11   Physical education should strive consistently to promote the idea that play belongs in the good life.
Jesse Feiring Williams
> Ibid., p.121.

12   Physical education should conduct its activities on the principle that the whole person is involved.
Jesse Feiring Williams
> Ibid., p.262.

13   Students of physical education should remember that the doctrines taught them in their professional school are not necessarily true.
Jesse Feiring Williams
> Ibid., p.324.

14   The focus of the individual should be in society, and not in his muscles.
Jesse Feiring Williams
> Ibid., p.363.

15   Physical education should provide meaningful experiences in which the pupil can succeed, not only in the school, but also in the recreational field at home and in the community.
Jesse Feiring Williams
> Ibid., p.414

POLITICS

1 Sport is alienating. It will disappear in a universal communist society.
Jean-Marie Brohm
Sport – A Prison of Measured Time: Essays by Jean-Marie Brohm, translated by Ian Fraser, 1978, p. 52.

2 The birth of world sport parallels the consolidation of imperialism.
Jean-Marie Brohm
Ibid., p. 175.

3 The institution of sport is geared into the mechanisms of the capitalist system.
Jean-Marie Brohm
Ibid., p. 176.

4 Sport symbolizes the international environment and is also a pragmatic tool of the environment.
Richard Espy
The Politics of the Olympic Games, 1979, p. 8.

5 If sport is to be physical education and if it is not that it is a triviality, it must be political. For education without politics is knowledge without purpose.
Geof Gleeson
British Journal of Physical Education, vol. 14, no. 5, Sep/Oct., 1983, p. 139.

6 Politics is the management of society, without politics there would be anarchy and chaos. Sport is a part of society, therefore politics must be a part of sport.
Geof Gleeson
Ibid.

7 Sports lovers still nurture the fond belief that sport can somehow be considered in a vacuum remote from life as a whole – in spite of the fact that all evidence and analysis of the way that international sport functions points to the contrary.
Peter Hain
> *Don't Play with Apartheid: The Background to the Stop the Seventy Tour Campaign*, 1971, p. 93.

8 A sporting system is the by-product of society and its political system, and it is just boyhood dreaming to suppose you can ever take politics out of sport.
Peter Hain
> *The Observer*, May 2, 1971.

9 The consequences of political influence in sport are beyond precise expression but not beyond conjecture.
J. M. Kilburn
> *Overthrows: A Book of Cricket*, 1975, p. 20.

10 Ninety-five per cent of my problems as President of the IOC involved national and international politics. . .
Lord Killanin
> *My Olympic Years*, 1983, p. 2.

11 The best performers anywhere want to test their skill against the best from elsewhere, but because at international level the best performer merges some of his identity in the nation itself, whether he wants to do so or not, success in sport has political importance.
P. C. McIntosh
> *Sport in Society*, 1963, p. 197.

12 Sport in the West has never been immune from the infiltration of political elements.
Alex Natan
> 'Sport and Politics', in John W. Loy Jr. and Gerald S. Kenyon (ed.), *Sport, Culture and Society*, 1969, p. 209.

13 To hold sport hostage to political purposes only serves to create new sources of conflict, for we lose irrevocably one of the

greatest opportunities open to us to meet in a friendly manner
and seek mutual understanding.
Juan Antonio Samaranch
(IOC President – In his address at the 1984 Olympic Games)
Quoted by John Rodda.

The Guardian, Jul. 26, 1984.

14 I maintain that the British tendency to put sport first and
politics second is a healthier tendency.
F. S. Smythe

Over Tyrolese Hills, 1936, p. 35.

POLO

1 Horse Hockey
Anonymous
(Early newspaper description of Polo)
Quoted by John Ford.

This Sporting Land, 1977, p. 188.

2 . . . freed from mundane cares in Bangalore in 1897 we devoted
ourselves to the serious purpose of life. This was expressed in
one word – Polo.
Winston Churchill

Ibid.

3 The polo mount is not a pony. It is a horse – a small horse to
be sure – but not a pony.
Harry Disston

Beginning Polo, 1973, p. 16.

4 The three basic essentials of success in polo are:
    1) a mount that is fast, handy, easily controlled, and not
       unduly excited;
    2) reliable and accurate stroking (hitting);
    3) effective team play.
Harry Disston

Ibid., p. 17.

POWERBOAT RACING

1   The boats are streamlined, advertisement-spattered, potential coffins, and are controlled on a knife-edge balance of courage and sense.
    Simon Barnes

The Times, Aug. 27, 1985.

2   The more boat you have in contact with the water, the slower you go. The less boat in contact with the water, then the more audible become the beating of the wings of the Angel of Death.
    Simon Barnes

Ibid.

3   There is no hope of bailing out of a speedboat. You hit the water and become so much pulp.
    Donald Campbell
    Quoted by Douglas Young-James.
        Donald Campbell: An Informal Biography, 1968, p. 62.

4   Scrutineers get all the kicks and few of the ha'pence of powerboat racing.
    Crab Searl

The Daily Telegraph – BP: Round Britain
Powerboat Race, 1970, p. 58.

PSYCHOLOGY

1   Sport is an aspect of Psychology. Psychology is an aspect of sport.
    Anonymous

2 The fat child, like the thin, learns that the playground gives rewards to the mesomorph and not to him.
G. W. Allport
Quoted by L. B. Hendry.
'The Coaching Stereotype', in H. T. A. Whiting (ed.),
Readings in Sports Psychology, 1972, p. 36.

3 Although physiological and circulatory limits to muscular exercise may be important, it is psychological factors beyond the ken of physiology which set this razor's edge between defeat and victory and which determine how closely an athlete comes to the absolute limits of performance.
Roger Bannister
Quoted by D. J. Glencross.
Psychology and Sport, 1978, preface.

4 The common belief that 'practice' makes perfect is not true. It is practice the results of which are known that makes perfect.
F. C. Bartlett
Quoted by D. J. Glencross.
Ibid., p. 97.

5 Physical education can be looked upon as a process through which an individual learns to appreciate psychologically the capacities of his body; what pleasures he can uniquely express through it and derive from it by means of motor activity.
L. Cooper
Quoted by H. T. A. Whiting.
'The Body Concept', in H. T. A. Whiting et al. (ed.),
*Personality and Performance in Physical Education
and Sport*, 1973, p. 43.

6 We perceive not only the motion of objects but also the movements of ourselves; the performance of fielding a baseball illustrates both . . .
J. J. Gibson
Quoted by G. J. K. Aldersen.
'Perceptual Studies: Variables Affecting the Perception
of Velocity in Sports Situations', in H. T. A. Whiting (ed.),
Readings in Sports Psychology, 1972, p. 128.

7 Using emotion effectively to push yourself or your team to the
peak of performance is desirable – but dangerous.
A. W. J. Hubbard
Quoted by H. T. A. Whiting.
                              'Psychology of Competition' in Ibid., p. 18.

8 Sport, as a mecca for man's competitive nature, cannot suddenly
become a place of mutual sharing.
H. Slusher
Quoted by L. B. Hendry.
                              'The Coaching Stereotype' Ibid., p. 47.

RACE/
DISCRIMINATION

1 For all its benefits, sport profits from failure: the failure of black
kids to integrate more satisfactorily, gain qualifications more
readily, find careers more easily.
Ernest Cashmore
                                        Black Sportsmen, 1982, p. 207.

2 Black people exist in perpetual struggle with mainstream
America about the nature of reality. And nowhere is this more
evident than in sports.
Harry Edwards
                                   The New York Times, May 6, 1979.

3 Whites control South Africa and Whites control South African
sport.
Peter Hain
                  *Don't Play with Apartheid: The Background to
the Stop the Seventy Tour Campaign*, 1971, p. 35.

4 The special role of sport in world society means that sport is at once apartheid's strongest arm and its potential foe.
Peter Hain

Ibid., p. 71.

5 Inhumanity to man is every man's concern.
Peter Hain

Ibid., p. 87.

6 Do not deceive yourself thinking that racialism is just another tyranny, like political tyranny, or religious tyranny. I know many men who have changed their religion, and many who have changed their politics. But I know of no man who has ever changed his race.
Albert Luthuli
Quoted by Peter Hain.

Ibid., p. 15.

7 Though racism and prejudice exist in sports, our sports people can hold their heads high. Over all, sports has done a better job at race relations than has any other field we can think of.
Herman L. Masin

Scholastic Coach, Oct., 1980, p. 19.

8 The domination of the black athlete in sports is not biological – it is derived from a complex nexus of historical, psychological and sociological forces surrounding the false hope that sports provide an opportunity to escape from the ghetto.
Ross Thomas Runfola

The New York Times, Feb. 27, 1977.

9 If I do something good then I am an American, but if I do something bad then I am a Negro!
Tommie Smith
(Winner of 200 metres, Mexico Olympics 1968)
Quoted by Christopher Brasher.
  Mexico 1968: A Diary of the XIXth Olympiad, 1968, p. 73.

10 Sport has increased the opportunities for the Negro to go to college. It must now make certain that what is inside that open door is more than a basketball court, a football play book – and a fast exit to oblivion.

Sports Illustrated (Editorial), Aug. 5, 1968, p. 9.

11   For Negro athletes in America, this is the Golden era, the halcyon day.
A. S. Young
          'Sports and the Negro', in George H. Sage (ed.),
Sports and American Society: Selected Readings, 1970, p. 274.

RAMBLING

1   Experience of walking and looking is the first step towards understanding and enjoying the countryside and is fundamental to outdoor education.
DES (Department of Education and Science)
          Movement: Physical Education in the Primary Years,
1972, p. 109.

2   Strictly speaking walking consists of putting one foot after the other and keeping upright at the same time.
Eric Leyland
                    The Open Air Is My Hobby, 1960, p. 3.

3   Like all sports, and walking is a sport if tackled the right way, rhythm is the first key.
Eric Leyland
                                        Ibid., p. 4.

4   You can't hit a cricket ball properly without rhythm, you can't play tennis or golf or ride a horse without it. Neither can you walk properly.
Eric Leyland
                                              Ibid.

5   To enjoy a countryside it is essential to make a direct contact with it, and this is only to be accomplished by walking over it.
F. S. Smythe
                    Over Tyrolese Hills, 1936, p. 280.

6   There is much more to walking than I ever suspected.
F. S. Smyth
                                        Ibid., p. 281.

7   Good walking comes of good balance.
    G. Winthrop Young
    In Sydney Spencer (ed.), *The Lonsdale Library*, Vol. 18, p. 48.

RECORDS/
RESULTS/STATISTICS

1   Say you were standing with one foot in the oven and one foot
    in an ice bucket. According to the percentage people, you
    should be perfectly comfortable.
    Bobby Bragan
    (On Statistics in Baseball)
    　　　　　'Scorecard', *Sports Illustrated*, Apr. 22, 1963, p. 12.

2   We remember not the scores and the results in after years; it
    is the men who remain in our minds, in our imagination.
    Neville Cardus
    　　　　　　　　　English Cricket, 1945, p. 11.

3   Sport is not only play and the making of records; it is likewise
    a soaring and a refreshment.
    Karl Jaspers
    　　　'Limits of the Life Order: Sport', in Ellen W. Gerber (ed.),
    Sport and the Body: A Philosophical Symposium, 1974, p. 119.

4   Memory does funny things, and chronological time becomes
    just as unimportant as final scores.
    J. Kendall-Carpenter
    　　　　　Rugby World, vol. 13, no. 3, Mar., 1973, p. 17.

5   Statistics are used like a drunk uses a lamp post – for support,
    not illumination.
    Vince Scully
    　　　　　'Coaches' Corner', *Scholastic Coach*, Jan., 1983, p. 77.

6 There are aspects to every athletic performance which are forever beyond the reach of any recording, because they take place in situations which A. are concrete, B. are subject to contingencies, C. involve novelties, D. are affected by luck, E. are beset by obstacles, and F. are benefited by opportunities.
Paul Weiss
'Records and the Man', in R. G. Osterhoudt (ed.),
The Philosophy of Sport: A Collection of
Original Essays, 1973, p. 15.

RELIGION

1 Pole vaulting is a religious experience.
Dr R. V. Ganslen
Mechanics of the Pole Vault, 1973, p. 5.

2 It is no longer simply the expression of self through space, it has become the modern religion of youth.
Geof Gleeson
(On Sport)
British Journal of Physical Education,
vol. 14, no. 5, Sep/Oct., 1983, p. 139.

3 There is no height, no depth, that the spirit of man, guided by a higher spirit, cannot attain.
Sir John Hunt
The Ascent of Everest, 1953, p. 232.

4 Our prayers should be for a sound mind in a healthy body.
Juvenal
Quoted by Frank S. Mead.
Encyclopedia of Religious Quotations, 1965, p. 211.

5 Everybody wants to go to heaven, but nobody wants to die.
Joe Louis
'Scorecard', *Sports Illustrated*, Jul. 19, 1965, p. 10.

6 The British have never been a spiritually minded people, so they invented cricket to give them some notion of eternity.
Lord Mancroft
> 'Scorecard', *Sports Illustrated*, Nov. 11, 1963, p. 16.

7 In its most majestic form sport aspires to the evincement of pure spirit obtained only by the purely religious act.
William Morgan
> 'An Existential Phenomenological Analysis of Sport as a Religious Experience', in R. G. Osterhoudt (ed.), *The Philosophy of Sport: A Collection of Original Essays*, 1973, p. 81.

8 Sports are religious in the sense that they are organized institutions, disciplines, and liturgies; and also in the sense that they teach religious qualities of heart and soul.
Michael Novak
> *The Joys of Sports*, 1976, p. 21.

9 Sport, rightly conceived, is an occupation carried out by the whole man. It renders the body a more perfect instrument of the soul and at the same time makes the soul itself a finer instrument of the whole man in seeking for Truth and in transmitting it to others. In this way it helps a man to reach that End to which all other ends are subordinate, the service and the greater glory of His Creator.
Pope Pius XII
(Addressing the Central School of Sports of the USA, Jul. 29, 1945)
Quoted by J. J. Twomey.
> *Christian Philosophy and Physical Education*, Strawberry Hill Booklets no. 1.

10 . . . Glorify God in your body . . .
The Bible
> 1 Corinthians, ch. 6, verse 20.

11 An horse is a vain thing for safety:
The Bible
> Psalm 33, verse 17.

12 For bodily exercise profiteth little: but godliness is profitable unto all things.
The Bible
> 1 Timothy, ch. 4, verse 8.

13 Sports always have been many things to many people, some-
    thing to all people. Even the most puritanical of early American
    settlers paused and watched sports long enough to decide that
    they were frivolous.
    A. S. Young
                    'Sports and the Negro', in George H. Sage (ed.),
        Sport and American Society: Selected Readings, 1970, p. 276.

ROWING

1 There can hardly be a sport that demands greater all-round
   physical perfection of its participants and produces, at its best,
   competition so aesthetically satisfying.
   David Hunn
   (On Rowing)
                            The Observer, Aug. 5, 1984, p. 34.

2 Henley is full of haughty happiness, hats, haves and very few
   have-nots.
   Frank Keating
                            The Guardian, Jul. 1, 1983, p. 22.

3 By far the greatest contributory factors to success are fitness
   and the will to win but it is upon its technique that the ultimate
   pace of the crew depends.
   Geoffrey Page
                            Coaching for Rowing, 1963, p. 10.

4 The functions of a rowing coach are firstly to teach individuals
   how to move a boat, secondly to weld together a number of
   these individuals into a crew, and thirdly to perfect the crew's
   fitness to race.
   A. C. Scott
               In a preface to J. P. G. Williams and A. C. Scott (ed.),
                        Rowing: A Scientific Approach, 1967.

5 Henley is now no longer a serious sporting event topped by a froth of young things dressed in boaters and Edwardian dress. It is now a full-scale British Day Out, a honeypot for the hoi-polloi in leisure wear.
Nicholas Wapshott

> *The Times*, Jun. 27, 1983, p. 7.

6 In the last analysis rowing is an affair of men and to each, if they are fortunate, will come one or more of those moments of truth when somehow man, oars, boat and water are perfectly integrated and the rowing transcends for a brief spell all normal experience.
J. P. G. Williams

> 'Rowing – Art of Science', in J. P. G. Williams and A. C. Scott (ed.), *Rowing: A Scientific Approach*, 1967, p. 20.

RUGBY LEAGUE

1 Rugby League is war without the frills.
Anonymous

2 To play Rugby League you need three things; a good pass, a good tackle and a good excuse.
Anonymous

3 Rugby League is as resilient as its players.
Keith Macklin

> *The Rugby League Game*, 1967, p. 11.

4 They are not all intellectuals, they are not all morons.
Keith Macklin
(On Rugby League Players)

> Ibid., p. 54.

5 There are grounds, and there are grounds.
Keith Macklin

> Ibid., p. 60.

6 Lighthouse keepers have a lonely job. So do referees.
Keith Macklin

Ibid., p. 75.

7 It's an up and under!
Eddie Waring
(Catch phrase)

8 No team can do well without good wingers, and no winger can
be considered really good unless he has genuine speed.
Eddie Waring
The Eddie Waring Book of Rugby League, 1966, p. 103.

RUGBY UNION

1 Strategy is the cutting of your coat according to your cloth.
Fred Allen
Quoted by Jim Wallace.
*The Rugby Game: A Manual for Coaches
and Players*, 1976, p. 9.

2 Show me a team with high-scoring wings – and I'll show you a
team with good centres.
Fred Allen

Ibid., p. 66.

3 The complexities of forward play conceal simplicities. The first
of these simplicities is body position.
Fred Allen

Ibid., p. 86.

4 This stone commemorates the exploit of William Webb Ellis,
who, with a fine disregard for the rules of football as played in
his time, first took the ball in his arms and ran with it, thus
originating the distinctive feature of the Rugby game. A.D.
1823.
Anonymous

(Plaque set in the wall at Rugby School.)

5 French Barbarians (a tautology if ever there was one).
   Simon Barnes
   The Times, Apr. 2, 1984, p. 19.

6 Forward play, sonny, is like a funeral. You have to get in front,
   with the family; not behind, with the friends . . .
   Michael Benazet
   Quoted by Dennis Lalanne.
   The Great Fight of the French Fifteen,
   translated by E. J. Boyd-Wilson, 1960, p. 1.

7 Rugby football is a game for gentlemen in all classes, but never
   for a bad sportsman in any class.
   Right Reverend W. J. Carey
   (Barbarians' motto on club flag)
   Quoted by Vivian Jenkins.
   Rugby World, vol. 13, no. 7, Jul., 1973, p. 4.

8 It would be a very dull game without individual brilliance, but
   it would cease to be a game if the whole team didn't benefit
   by it.
   Peter Cranmer
   Rugby Football: An Anthology, compiled by Kenneth
   Pelmear in collaboration with J. E. Morpurgo, 1958, p. 353.

9 The hand-off is a circumscribed blow; . . .
   Scott Crawford
   British Journal of Physical Education,
   vol. 7, no. 6, Nov./Dec., 1976, p. 204.

10 The pub is as much a part of rugby as the playing field.
   J. Dickinson
   A Behavioural Analysis of Sport, 1976, p. 43.

11 A forward's usefulness to his side varies as to the square of his
   distance from the ball.
   Clarrie Gibbons
   Quoted by Jim Wallace.
   *The Rugby Game: A Manual for Coaches
   and Players*, 1976, p. 147.

12 A game played by fewer than fifteen a side, at least half of whom should be totally unfit.
Michael Green
(Definition of Coarse Rugby.)
The Art of Coarse Rugby or *Any Number Can Play* (1960),
1975.

13 Rugger is a game for the fit, the enthusiastic, the young men with energy to burn. Coarse Rugby is played by those who are too old, too young, too light, too heavy, too weak, too lazy, too slow, too cowardly or too unfit for ordinary rugger.
Michael Green

Ibid., p. 17.

14 The basis of all rugby is fitness; without it, skill and understanding are all but useless.
J. T. Greenwood

Improve Your Rugby, 1967, p. 11.

15 A major rugby tour by the British Isles to New Zealand is a cross between a medieval crusade and a prep school outing.
John Hopkins

*Life with the Lions: The Inside Story of
the 1977 New Zealand Tour*, 1977, p. 1.

16 Rugby football is first and foremost about attitudes. Unless the approach is right, the basics and the skills will suffer and no values of any dimension, least of all aesthetic, will be achieved.
Carwyn James

The Sunday Times, Oct. 22, 1972.

17 Rucking is New Zealand's greatest contribution to the game of Rugby.
Carwyn James
Quoted by Jim Wallace.

*The Rugby Game: A Manual for Coaches
and Players*, 1976, p. 141.

18 'The one-handed "palmer" can always reach higher', they say. They may be right, but the result is that nearly every line-out is like a tropical island – all waving palms.
Vivian Jenkins

Rugby World, vol. 9, no. 11, Nov., 1969, p. 4.

19　There are two kinds of Rugby . . . the Rugby of ambition, bound up with winning, and crowds and caps, and supporters; and the Rugby of personal enjoyment, which concerns what the player himself gets out of the game. The two things do not always mix, although they can.
Vivian Jenkins
Rugby World, vol. 13, no. 7, Jul., 1973, p. 3.

20　The one implies try your damnest, but without rancour; the other says win at all costs, and hate your opponents' guts.
Vivian Jenkins
(On the difference between healthy and unhealthy rivalry.)
Ibid.

21　A prop's first duty lies in the scrummage. If he can run and handle as well, so much the better. If he can do everything, of course, you have a champion.
Vivian Jenkins
Rugby World, vol. 14, no. 2, Feb., 1974, p. 4.

22　The essentials that go to make a good coach are (a) attitude, (b) technical knowledge, and (c) the ability to motivate players, and I regard the ability to motivate as the most important.
Cliff Jones
Quoted by Vivian Jenkins.
Rugby World, vol. 11, no. 3, Mar., 1971, p. 19.

23　In quaint, friendly New Zealand – where church is low, tea is high and brows are middling – rugby football is the enduring passion.
Frank Keating
Up and Under: A Rugby Diary, 1983, p. 161.

24　Beer and Rugby are more or less synonymous.
Chris Laidlaw
*Mud in Your Eye: A Worm's Eye View
of the Changing World of Rugby*, 1973, p. 8.

25　In Welsh valleys Rugby is more than an amusement, it is a whole social order.
Chris Laidlaw
Ibid.

26 With the passing of British Rugby into the same emotional zone as that occupied by the New Zealand and South African game, losing takes on a new bitter significance.
Chris Laidlaw

Ibid., p. 11.

27 Rugby may have many problems but the gravest is undoubtedly that of the persistence of summer.
Chris Laidlaw

Ibid., p. 12.

28 Rugby has always captured the imagination of the French, just as the French have always captured the imagination in their Rugby.
Chris Laidlaw

Ibid., p. 174.

29 A trial match is not a Rugby match. It is just the opposite. It is a calamity.
Dennis Lalanne

La Mêlée Fantastique, translated by
E. J. Boyd-Wilson, 1962, p. 32.

30 You are either a Rugbyman or you are not one.
Dennis Lalanne

Ibid., p. 99.

31 I believe that belote, bowls, politics, love, religion, urban housing, the atomic bomb, the war in Algeria and potato chips do not fill the thoughts of people in France as much as Rugby stirs the souls of New Zealanders.
Dennis Lalanne

Ibid., p. 124.

32 Rugby demands from men not only their minds, their spontaneity and their endurance. It demands the best that is in them, to their very last gasp.
Dennis Lalanne

The Great Fight of the French Fifteen,
translated by E. J. Boyd-Wilson, 1960, p. 17.

33 . . . Rugby is not like tea, which is good only in England, with English water and English milk. On the contrary, Rugby would

be better, frankly, if it were made in a Twickenham pot and warmed up in a Pyrenean cauldron.
Dennis Lalanne

Ibid., p. 21.

34 No Rugby revolution can come about, no new ambitious back play can be perfected, without what will always remain the basis of victory or defeat – scrumwork.
Dennis Lalanne
Quoted by Jim Wallace.

The Rugby Game: A Manual for Coaches and Players, 1976, p. 97.

35 Listen . . .! . . . It's a Goal!
Winston McCarthy

Book title and catch phrase.

36 If genius be described as the power of light striking through the gloom, then Nepia was that light.
Terry McLean

Introduction in George Nepia and Terry McLean,
I, George Nepia: The Golden Years of Rugby Football,
1963, p. 10.

37 A touring team, especially an unbeaten one on a long tour, is the Aunt Sally of the rugby world in which it is travelling.
Maxwell Price

Springboks in the Lions Den, 1961, p. 11.

38 There is of course something special about England as far as rugby is concerned. After all, they invented the game.
Wallace Reyburn
The Men in White: The Story of English Rugby, 1975, p. 9.

39 The laws of the game are written down for all to see. There may be a lot of secrets about how to win, but there is no secret about how to play.
Derek Robinson

Rugby: Success Starts Here, 1969, intro.

40 It's the players who benefit from the laws, so it's up to the players to apply them.
Derek Robinson

Ibid.

41   The Advantage Law is the best law in the book, because it lets you ignore all the others for the good of the game.
Derek Robinson

Ibid., p. 135.

42   To play Rugger well you must play it fiercely, and at the same time, and all the time, remember while doing so that you are a gentleman.
E. H. D. Sewell
Rugger: The Man's Game, revised by O. L. Owen (1944), 1950, p. 22.

43   There are four kinds of tries: the Combined Try, the Individual Try, the Gift Try, the Invalid Try.
E. H. D. Sewell

Ibid., p. 92.

44   Lanky folk, unless they have the loins for the job, are very rarely good kickers.
E. H. D. Sewell

Ibid., p. 104.

45   Captains have to work hard to maintain a standard: they have to keep their committees happy, appease the supporters' clubs, attend all training sessions, study the opposition, make diplomatic speeches and be above reproach themselves.
J. B. G. Thomas
Rugby World, vol. 13, no. 8, Aug., 1973, p. 32.

46   All the problems of sevens arise from the basic fact of space.
Mike Williams
Rugby Sevens, 1975, p. 22.

47   Rugby sevens is a possession game and it is a pressure game – the link between the two is support.
Mike Williams

Ibid., p. 31.

48   Standards in Rugby football are governed by three factors: participation, competition, and coaching.
Ray Williams
Skilful Rugby, 1976, p. 37.

49 If winning possession is to be regarded as the foundation stone of the game, then using it should be regarded as the superstructure.
Ray Williams

Ibid., p. 115.

50 . . . disappearing fast is the old rugby school complex, with its disciplined young spectators toeing the line with a verbal show of esprit de corps.
Wilfred Wooller

Rugby World, vol. 11, no. 2, Feb., 1971, p. 9.

51 Man is a fighting animal and Rugby is a civilised (almost always, anyway) blood sport.
Wilfred Wooller

Rugby World, vol. 11, no. 12, Dec., 1971, p. 9.

SHOOTING (TARGET)

1 No shot is big enough to stop a target without hitting it.
A. H. Bogardus
Quoted by Chris Cradock.

A Manual of Clayshooting, 1983, p. 60.

2 The art of seeing lead should always be cultivated.
Chris Cradock

Ibid., p. 61.

3 Pistol Shooting, indeed all target shooting, is now a sport in its own right, no longer an adjunct of the military art.
P. C. Freeman
Target Pistol Shooting: Eliminating the Variables, 1981, intro.

4 Pistol shooting is not a number of separate actions but the co-ordination and fusion of the parts.
P. C. Freeman

Ibid., p. 60.

5 The requisites for successful shooting are a rifle which will shoot
straight, ammunition which performs consistently and an ability
in the marksman to make good use of them.
W. H. Fuller
Small-Bore Target Shooting, revised by A. J. Palmer, 1968,
p. 11.

6 Target shooting is not a black art – it is fundamentally a mechanical and physical exercise.
W. H. Fuller

Ibid., p. 12.

7 There is no substitute for placing the pattern on the target.
W. W. Greener
Quoted by Chris Cradock.

A Manual of Clayshooting, 1983, p. 60.

SKIING

1 Skiing . . . aesthetically gratifying, technically demanding, and
bracingly elemental.
David Boroff
'A View of Skiers as a Subculture', in J. W. Loy Jr.
and G. S. Kenyon (ed.), *Sport, Culture, and Society*, 1969,
p. 455.

2 It is not a jumping sport. It is a flying sport: a lifting sport.
Shirley Finberg-Sullivan
(On ski-jumping)
Quoted by E. M. Swift.

Sports Illustrated, Feb. 4, 1980, p. 34.

3 There are no natural jumpers, because what they do is so
unnatural.
Shirley Finberg-Sullivan
(On ski-jumping)
Quoted by E. M. Swift.

Ibid., p. 38.

4 Skiing is a battle against yourself, always to the frontiers of the impossible. But most of all, it must give you pleasure. It is not an obligation but a joy.
Jean-Claude Killy
Sports Illustrated, Nov. 18, 1968, p. 57.

5 Ski jumping is not speed and spring against gravity; the jumpers are kitelike, riding on air.
E. M. Swift
Sports Illustrated, Feb. 4, 1980, p. 36.

6 . . . skiing draws us into a tense and moving play about ourselves and our lives. It would be a poor play indeed – and it would certainly not be about our lives – if it ever lost its most dramatic and spell-binding quality, the quality of danger – real, genuine, leg-breaking danger.
G. H. Weltner
Quoted by Roselyn E. Stone.
'Perceptual Studies: Sources and Kinds of Meaning
in The Acts of Surfing and Skiing',
in H. T. A. Whiting (ed.), *Readings in Sports Psychology*,
1972, p. 185.

SKILL

1 Mass-scale sport is the underpinnings of expertise.
Andrei Batashev
Sport in the USSR, Oct., 1983, p. 35.

2 The main function of sport is that it serves as a basis for the exercise of skill, with physical prowess.
R. Carlisle
'Physical Education and Aesthetics', in H. T. A. Whiting and
D. W. Masterson (ed.), *Readings in the Aesthetics
of Sport*, 1974, p. 24.

3 The growth of skill comes largely as a result of the challenges within the game, no matter how simple it is.
DES (Department of Education and Science)
Movement: Physical Education in the Primary Years, 1972, p. 76.

4 . . . the ability to execute a pattern of behavioural elements in proper relation to a certain environment and this can be further stated as skill = speed × accuracy × form × adaptability.
Harry W. Johnson
(Definition of Skill)
Quoted by P. C. Freeman.
Target Pistol Shooting: Eliminating the Variables, 1981, p. 72.

5 Technical excellence, however great, is all but useless, unless fired by the dynamism of the human spirit.
A. J. (Tony) O'Reilly
Foreword in E. S. Higham and W. J. Higham, *High Speed Rugby*, 1960.

SOCIETY

1 For what do we live, but to make sport for our neighbours, and laugh at them in our turn?
Jane Austen
Pride and Prejudice, ch. 1.

2 Without play and recreation it is impossible to develop good citizenship.
Henry A. Barker
Quoted by Thomas Curley.
'Playgrounds as Laboratories of Social Service and Civil Betterment', *Hygiene and Physical Education*, vol. 1, no. 1, Mar., 1909.

3 The concepts and language of sports are so familiar and pervasive that they are used as metaphors to clarify other aspects of American life.
Arnold Beisser
The Madness in Sport, 1977, p. 9.

4 Man's play is less governed by rationality than most activities, and attempts at intellectual analysis of its forms and motives find it hard to avoid the impression of being either patronizing or disparaging.
D. Brailsford
Sport and Society: Elizabeth to Anne, 1969, p. 5.

5 Physical activity and sport are basic and universal elements within virtually all cultures from highly industrialized societies to developing countries.
Albert V. Carron
Social Psychology of Sport, 1980, p. 1.

6 It cannot de denied, I think, that sports and games are now a necessity of civilisation.
Norman Clark
How to Box, 1931, p. 2;

7 Cultures have seen fit to reinforce sport or punish it or ignore it.
J. Dickinson
A Behavioural Analysis of Sport, 1976, p. 29.

8 Sports are utilitarian in product but not necessarily in process.
Harry Edwards
Sociology of Sport, 1973, p. 56.

9 The athlete's role in sports is characterized by powerlessness in terms of decision-making authority.
Harry Edwards
Ibid., p. 176.

10 In every society, sport not only reflects but also reinforces and reaffirms the prevailing character of human relations and the values of dominant group members.
Harry Edwards
The New York Times, May 6, 1979.

11 A lasting adolescent passion for football, an early-established interest in cricket, boxing, tennis, athletics, help to keep the flame alight, but it is the point at which sport makes some kind of comment on the human situation which is truly memorable; and valuable.
Brian Glanville
The Sunday Times, Sep. 25, 1983.

12 Culture is an essential part of any society, it is the conveyor of past values to the future through the modifier of the present. Sport should be, and must be, a part of that culture.
Geof Gleeson

> *British Journal of Physical Education,*
> vol. 14, no. 5, Sep./Oct., 1983, p. 139.

13 The moment sport becomes a utilitarian activity practiced for profit it loses its connection with leisure from which it originally sprang and which gives it its essential dignity and its close affinity with culture.
René Maheu

> 'Cultural Anthropology', in E. Jokl and E. Simon (ed.),
> *International Research in Sport and Physical Education*, 1964,
> p. 11.

14 At the beginning of the twentieth century, the Ivy League athlete who combined sporting proficiency with stiff character and the proper social credentials was a bona fide American hero.
Christian Messenger

> 'Tom Buchanan and the Demise of the Ivy League
> Athletic Hero', *Journal of Popular Culture*, 1974/5.

15 Sport is used by the Party as a lever of social control, offering the Soviet regime a wonderful opportunity to exploit genuine enthusiasm and at the same time channel leisure-time activity toward party-inspired goals.
Henry W. Morton

> *Soviet Sport: Mirror of Soviet Society*, 1963, p. 22.

16 Sports are not, of course, all of life. What good are courage, honesty, freedom, community, and excellence if they do not inform one's family life, civil life, political life, work life?
Michael Novak

> *The Joys of Sports*, 1976, p. 42.

17 Sports are the highest products of civilization and the most accessible, lived, experiential sources of the civilizing spirit.
Michael Novak

> Ibid., p. 43.

18 Those who have contempt for sports, our serious citizens, are a danger to the human race, ants among men, drones in the honeycomb.
Michael Novak

Ibid.

19 To diagnose sports as the source of machismo is like diagnosing love as the source of selfishness.
Michael Novak

Ibid., p. 45.

20 If life is not a football game, neither is it a morality play . . .
Michael Novak

The New York Times, Jan. 30, 1977.

21 Sport was born of man's highest ideals and has been around for 33 centuries, which is longer than any religion, culture or sub-culture; it must be defended and harnessed for its values.
Ron Pickering

Quoted in *Action: British Journal of Physical Education*, vol. 13, no. 4, Jul., 1982, p. 118.

22 If all the year were playing holidays,
To sport would be as tedious as to work.
William Shakespeare

(Henry, Prince of Wales), *First Part of King Henry the Fourth*, act I, sc. II, l. 226.

23 In essence, sport is a natural laboratory for dissecting and laying open for observation many workings of a society and its culture. This mirroring of society takes place on several levels . . . and it includes . . . stability and change, consensus and conflict, normative and deviant behaviour, reality and unreality, success and defeat, heroes and villains, ecstasy and agony.
Eldon E. Snyder

Journal of Popular Culture.

24 The sociological analysis of sport has significance far beyond the institution of sport itself.
Eldon E. Snyder

Ibid.

25   Sport, far from being limited to the gymnasium, pool and playing fields, embraces the whole complex of human dynamics and can be used as one vehicle by which the oneness and diversity of mankind may be developed, practiced and preserved in an atmosphere of trust and growth.
     Dale P. Toohey
               'Sport Sociology – The Comparative and International
                         Dimension', in Comparative Physical Education
                    and Sport, proceedings of an International Seminar,
               Wingate Institute, Netanya – Israel, Dec., 1978, p. 159.

26   The English passion for the amusements which are technically called 'sports', is as strong in these colonies as it is at home.
     A. Trollope
               'Australian Sports', in T. D. Jaques and G. R. Pavia (ed.),
                              *Sport in Australia, Selected Readings in
                                              Physical Activity*, p. 24.

27   For an outsider, a taste of local sport often provides a useful entrée into the style of local life.
     James Walvin
     The People's Game: A Social History of British Football, 1975,
                                                              p. 2.

28   The athletic goal rarely allows a man to work toward the achievement of anyone but himself, except incidentally and as a means.
     Paul Weiss
               'Records and the Man', in R. G. Osterhoudt (ed.),
                         *The Philosophy of Sport: A Collection of
                                      Original Essays*, 1973, p. 23.

29   I love sport because I love life, and sport is one of the basic joys of life.
     Yevgeny Yevtushenko
                              Sports Illustrated, Dec. 19, 1966, p. 128.

SPECTATORS

1 Fans are fickle.
Bryant J. Cratty
Social Psychology in Athletics, 1981, p. 280.

2 Which is the more enviable lot for the onlooker at a game – to
care too much who wins or not to care at all?
Bernard Darwin
'Let the Better Side Lose', in Peter Ryde (ed.),
Mostly Golf: A Bernard Darwin Anthology, 1976, p. 54.

3 Perhaps if the game of football itself had a stronger moral
content, it could raise better defences against those who turn
its arenas into cockpits of ignobility.
Russell Davies
The Sunday Times, Aug. 28, 1983.

4 The philosophy of hooliganism ends with a kick in the face.
(Title of an article by Dudley Doust)
The Sunday Times: Sports Book, 1979, p. 76.

5 – A shrieking, whistling, fire-cracking mass of bias –
David Lacey
(Description of Roma football supporters)
The Guardian, Apr. 27, 1984.

6 There is only one emotion that I know of which has absolutely
no place in spectator sport and death to it – laughter.
René Maheu
'Cultural Anthropology', in E. Jokl and E. Simon (ed.),
*International Research in Sport and
Physical Education*, 1964, p. 13.

7 Spectators' sports found lodgement in American society earlier
than did those in which participation is the price of enjoyment.
Frederic L. Paxson
'The Rise of Sport', in George H. Sage (ed.),
Sport and American Society: Selected Readings, 1970, p. 21.

8 The superfan has a primary need for identification with the football team: sitting on the bench, hanging around the locker room, calling the football stars by their first names – these are all wish-fulfillments.
George Plimpton
Sports Illustrated, Sep. 13, 1965, p. 109.

9 Because the spectator cannot experience what the athlete is experiencing, the fan is seldom a good loser.
George Sheehan
Dr Sheehan on Running, 1978, p. 193.

SPORT

1 What is sport? I suppose it's anything they can make competitive or entertaining enough to be good television.
Anonymous
The Observer, Aug. 22, 1982.

2 Sport is a lifelong ticket to a private theatre in which the player can act out as many roles as he likes. He can play the daring attacker or the dependable defender, the high-risk entrepreneur or the subtle tactician.
Andrew Bailey
Future Sport, 1982, p. 23.

3 There is something for everyone in sports.
Arnold Beisser
'Modern Man and Sports', in George H. Sage (ed.), *Sport and American Society: Selected Readings*, 1970, p. 239.

4 Sport is adventure, personal and vicarious.
R. Brasch
How Did Sports Begin?: A Look into the Origins of Man at Play, 1973.

5 Sport is any game or recreation played to a set of rules. A
fisherman sitting on a bank is indulging in a recreation until he
does it competitively; aeromodelling is a recreation but put
some rules on it and it becomes a sport.
Christopher Brasher

The Observer, Aug. 22, 1982.

6 The fact that sport is basically non-rational is not always evident
to those who are totally absorbed in it.
Jan Broekhoff

'Sport and Ethics in the Context of Culture',
in R. G. Osterhoudt (ed.), *The Philosophy of Sport:
A Collection of Original Essays*, 1973, p. 221.

7 Fraternity is a big part of sport.
Tamara Bykova

Sport in the USSR, Oct., 1983, p. 3.

8 The ideal of sport is built on determination and abnegation. As
a rule an effort is never lost.
Georges Carpentier

The Art of Boxing, 1926, p. 34.

9 In its highest aspect the sporting spirit is one of the simplest
yet most effective moralities known to mankind.
Norman Clark

How to Box, 1931, p. 7.

10 Sport is an institutionalised competitive activity that involves
physical exertion or the use of relatively complex skills by an
individual whose participation is motivated by a combination of
intrinsic satisfaction associated with the activity itself and the
external rewards earned through participation.
J. J. Coakley

Sport in Society; Issues and Controversies, 1978.

11 Sport is a highly charged, achievement-laden situation, one in
which an individual or a group performance is compared not
only to the performance of others, but also to absolute standards
of height, speed, distance, and time.
Bryant J. Cratty

Social Psychology in Athletics, 1981, p. 129.

12 Sport includes many diverse forms of behaviour, from highly cerebral games of strategy to the application of maximal force in a single response.
J. Dickinson
A Behavioural Analysis of Sport, 1976, p. 25.

13 One characteristic of all sports is that they require gross physical movement.
J. Dickinson
Ibid., p. 70.

14 Each sport resembles some others in certain respects, but there is no one property or group of properties possessed in common by every sport by virtue of which each of these activities is a sport.
R. K. Elliott
'Aesthetics and Sport', in H. T. A. Whiting and D. W. Masterson (ed.), *Readings in the Aesthetics of Sport*, 1974, p. 107.

15 There are few words in the English language which have such a multiplicity of divergent meaning as the word sport.
H. Graves
'A Philosophy of Sport', in Ellen W. Gerber (ed.), *Sport and the Body: A Philosophical Symposium*, 1974, p. 6.

16 There is no realm of human activity about which it is more difficult to think clearly than sport.
H. A. Harris
Sport in Britain: Its Origins and Development, 1975, p. 11.

17 The whole aim of any sport is to prove that on a particular day you can beat someone else at that sport.
Dick Hawkey
Winning Squash, 1976, p. 7.

18 Sport can be cruel to men.
Arthur Hopcraft
The Football Man, 1970, p. 11.

19 It is the uncertainty in sport which gives it much of its drama.
Arthur Hopcraft
Ibid., p. 95.

20 Sport – any competitive activity demanding skill and frequent physical exertion, the result of which may be decided without recourse to judgement.
David Hunn

The Observer, Aug. 22, 1982.

21 Sport is in the eyes of the beholder and in my view it is best left at that simplistic interpretation.
Peter Lawson

Ibid.

22 Sports is, or should be, just one of the things people do – an integral part of life, but only one aspect of it.
Robert Lipsyte

'Peddling Sports Myths: A Disservice to Young Readers', in *Interracial Books for Children Bulletin*, vol. 12, no. 1, 1981.

23 Sport is a stone of many facets.
Peter McIntosh

Fair Play: Ethics in Sport and Education, 1979, p. 153.

24 Those who know little about either like to see parallels between war and sports.
Drew Middleton

The New York Times, May 8, 1977.

25 Sport is an exportable commodity, like language and cuisine.
Andrew Mulligan

'Scorecard', *Sports Illustrated*, Dec. 20, 1965, p. 20.

26 Sport is a contest of physical strength or manipulation or more probably both (if it involves mental agility, so much the better, but that's no criterion).
Geoffrey Nicholson

The Observer, Aug. 22, 1982.

27 Sport is life to the nth degree.
Neil Offen
Quoted by Richard Lipsky.

National Forum, Winter, 1982.

28   If Sebastian Coe is running against High Wycombe's third string 800 metres man, that's not sport. But if Coe is running against Ovett, that's sport.
Dick Palmer
The Observer, Aug. 22, 1982.

29   It would appear that the problem of definition lies primarily in the field of semantics as the word 'sport' has been so widely used that any exact meaning which the term may have had has been eroded.
John Pearson
Action: British Journal of Physical Education,
vol. 13, no. 3, May, 1982, p. 82.

30   All sports are games of inches.
Dick Ritger
The New York Times, Apr. 17, 1977.

31   Sport is an activity that may contain one or more elements of play but is particularly characterised by components of skill, competition and the desire to achieve.
R. S. Rivenes
Foundations of Physical Education, 1978.

32   Sport is a school of honest competition, of doing one's best.
N. Terekhov
Sport in the USSR, Jan., 1983, p. 3.

33   Sports are a form of recreation, a way, literally, of recreating ourselves. They should enable us to relax and enjoy ourselves, to find new meanings in life, to get a different perspective on our jobs, our families, and the things we think are important. They should encourage us to participate and keep our own bodies ('a temple in which resides the soul') healthy, lean, and firm.
Gus Turbeville
'On Being Good Sports in Sports', in Ellen W. Gerber (ed.),
Sport and the Body: A Philosophical Symposium, 1974,
p. 255.

34   The attraction of sport lies in its creative essence.
Yuri Vlasov
Sport in the USSR, Jun., 1979, p. 18.

35 . . . true sport is always a duel: a duel with nature, with one's own fear, with one's own fatigue, a duel in which body and mind are strengthened.
Yevgeny Yevtushenko
Sports Illustrated, Dec. 19, 1966, p. 112.

SPORTSMANSHIP

1 Friendship first, competition second.
Anonymous
(Chinese Motto)

2 Always play a game with somebody, never against them. Always win a game, never beat an opponent.
Andrew Bailey
Future Sport, 1982, p. 32.

3 Playing a cheater is the real test of sportsmanship.
Jack Barnaby
Winning Squash Racquets, 1979, p. 210.

4 I care not who makes the laws or even writes the songs if the code of sportsmanship is sound, for it is that which controls conduct and governs the relationship between men.
Marcus Tullius Cicero
Quoted by Carle Willgoose.
The Curriculum in Physical Education, 1979, p. 61.

5 I've been thinking a lot about 'sportsmanship'. It's hard to define – especially in football, which starts with premeditated mayhem.
Pat Culpepper (Texas Linebacker)
(On receiving the Swede Nelson Sportsmanship Award)
'Scorecard', *Sports Illustrated*, Jan. 21, 1963, p. 9.

6   Nice guys finish last.
Leo Durocher (Attributed)

7   It is in Homer that we first find the true spirit of sport, the
desire to be ever the best and to excel all other men, the joy
in effort.
E. N. Gardiner
Athletics of the Ancient World, 1930, p. 18.

8   Sport is only really worth doing, if it is done with joy and
unselfishness.
Geof Gleeson
All About Judo, 1980, p. 61.

9   . . . sportsmanship, if true, remains untainted by inhumanity,
and is never brutalised by callousness.
F. W. Hackwood
Old English Sports, 1907, p. 24.

10 Almost everyone interested in the world of sport agrees that
all is not well with it.
H. A. Harris
Sport in Britain: Its Origins and Development, 1975, p. 9.

11 Today it is unfashionable to say so, but it nevertheless remains
true, that the greatest gift of those Victorian pioneers to sport
was their insistence on the importance of being a good loser.
H. A. Harris
Ibid., p. 212.

12 Sportsmanship, next to the Church, is the greatest teacher of
morals.
Herbert Hoover
Quoted by John Rickards Betts.
America's Sporting Heritage: 1850–1950, 1974, p. 357.

13 Justice does not always triumph in sports. Sometimes it's lucky
to gain even a tie. And sometimes it can go down like the
Titanic.
Herman L. Masin
Scholastic Coach, Apr., 1983.

14 (Sportsmanship) It means being a little more generous to an opponent than the rules of the game or even the idea of fair play demand; but only a little more generous – not in any demonstrative way and certainly not in any way that will imply patronage or take the keen edge off the competition.
R. E. Morgan
> *Concerns and Values in Physical Education*, 1974, p. 79.

15 In time I discovered that there is just as much satisfaction to be gained from honourable defeat as from meritorious victory.
Hennie Muller
> *Tot Siens to Test Rugby*, 1954, p. 211.

16 Sportsmanship is not a question of habits, not of a row of virtues, but of the union of I and you into we.
K. Rysdorp
> 'Competition As A Road to Education', in L. M. Fraley et al. (ed.), *Physical Education and Healthful Living*, 1954.

17 If thou dost play with him at any game
Thou art sure to lose, and, of that natural luck,
He beats thee 'gainst the odds;
William Shakespeare
> (A Soothsayer), *Antony and Cleopatra*, act II, sc. III, l. 25.

18 Players of sport should also be sportsmen.
John Underwood
> *Sports Illustrated*, Aug. 21, 1978, p. 32.

SQUASH RACKETS

1 Technique is the servant of tactics.
Jack Barnaby
> *Winning Squash Racquets*, 1979, p. 11.

2 Squash racquets is above all a percentage game.
Jack Barnaby
> Ibid., p. 25.

3 The essence of squash could, with care, be written on the back
   of a postage stamp. But one can spend a lifetime failing to
   master it.
   Rex Bellamy

   The Story of Squash, 1978, p. 3.

4 A stroke is a shot aimed at the ball!
   Dick Hawkey

   Winning Squash, 1976, p. 15.

5 Crystallising my feelings about the game, I find that squash is
   less frustrating than golf, less fickle than tennis. It is easier than
   badminton, cheaper than polo. It is better exercise than bowls,
   quicker than cricket, less boring than jogging, drier than swimming, safer than hang gliding.
   John Hopkins

   Squash: A Joyful Game, 1980, p. 1.

6 Squash is possibly atavistic in the way it appeals to our basic
   instincts.
   John Hopkins

   Ibid., p. 7.

7 Not so many moons ago, watching squash rackets was a bit like
   a home movie show of the family hols. Everyone in the audi-
   ence knew the actors and a reasonable crowd was about 25.
   David Miller

   The Times, Apr. 10, 1984.

SURFING

1 This is the essence of surfing, the delicate balance between
   control and chaos, and it works on surfers like a drug.
   E. Burdick
   Quoted by Roselyn E. Stone.
     'Perceptual Studies: Sources and Kinds of Meaning in the
       Acts of Surfing and Skiing', in H. T. A. Whiting (ed.),
         Readings in Sports Psychology, 1972, p. 185.

2 The surfer projects himself upon the wave as the matador before
   the bull . . .
   W. Cleary
   Quoted by Roselyn E. Stone.

                                                              Ibid.

3 What is surfing? Is it a sport, an art form, a personal involvement between man and the elements? Perhaps it touches, even
   if it fails to combine, all three.
   Reginald J. Prytherch
                        Surfing: A Modern Guide, 1972, p. 15.

4 Big-wave riding was, is and probably always will be something
   else. So were, are and probably always will be its
   practitioners, . . .
   Gilbert Rogin
          Sports Illustrated, vol. 23, no. 6, Oct. 18, 1965, p. 104.

SWIMMING

1 In swimming, possibly more than in any other sport, a person
   remembers that he is a child of nature.
   Anonymous
                           Sport in the USSR, Jun., 1980, p. 20.

2 Swimming as a systematic exercise is of doubtful good, and is
   attended by many dangers.
   James Cantlie
                           Physical Efficiency, 1906, p. 195.

3 The development of the crawl stroke is the history of Man's
   efforts to swim better and faster.
   Cecil Colwin
                    Cecil Colwin on Swimming, 1969, p. 17.

4 Man is not a swimming animal.
   Harold T. Friermood
           'The Need for Aquatic Research', in *Aquatics Guide*,
                                   Jul. 1963–Jul. 1965, p. 22.

5 The in-focus trainer has flexibility.
   Harry Gallagher
   Sprint the Crawl, 1976, p. 9.

6 Swimming is for everyone – for survival, for fitness and for fun.
   Peter Heatley
   Foreword in N. W. Sarsfield, *Swimming for Everyone*, 1965,
   p. 15.

7 Swimming gives scope for every type of temperament and
   talent, athletic and aesthetic.
   Sid G. Hedges
   Swimming is for Everyone, 1967, p. 11.

8 Since the very principle of a race is not the performance but
   victory, competition is the substance, the raison d'être of
   swimming.
   François Oppenheim
   The History of Swimming, 1970, p. 1.

9 Swimming is, more than any other physical exercise, a reversal
   to the primitive.
   John Boyle O'Reilly
   Ethics of Boxing and Manly Sport, 1888, p. 83.

10 The swimmer has no thoughts – only perceptions.
    John Boyle O'Reilly
    Ibid.

11 It is the swimmer and not the water which moves.
    N. W. Sarsfield
    Swimming for Everyone, 1965, p. 25.

12 As two spent swimmers, that do cling together
    And choke their art.
    William Shakespeare
    (A Sergeant), *Macbeth*, act I, sc. II, l. 8.

13 . . . Leander the good swimmer.
    William Shakespeare
    (Benedick), *Much Ado about Nothing*, act V, sc. II, l. 30.

14 . . . Or sink or swim.
   William Shakespeare
   (Hotspur), *The First Part of King Henry the Fourth*, act I,
   sc. III, l. 194.

15 Like an unpractis'd swimmer plunging still,
   With too much labour drowns for want of skill . . .
   William Shakespeare
   The Rape of Lucrece, l. 1098.

16 (*Stephano*), Here: swear then, how thou escapedst
   (*Trinculo*), Swam ashore, man, like a duck: I can swim like a
   duck, I'll be sworn.
   (*Stephano*), Here, kiss the book
   Though thou canst swim like a duck,
   thou art made like a goose.
   William Shakespeare
   The Tempest, act II, sc. II, l. 136.

SYNCHRONIZED SWIMMING

1 Synchronized swimming is skilful, challenging and fun, and
   combines watermanship with aesthetic appreciation.
   Helen Elkington
   Action: British Journal of Physical Education,
   vol. 13, no. 2, Mar., 1982, p. 41.

2 This afternoon a girl with a plastic smile and gelatined hair will
   win the penultimate gold of the Games. It will be awarded for
   an outstanding performance in holding your breath under water
   and waggling your legs in the air.
   David Hunn
   (On the introduction of synchronized swimming into the
   Olympic Games)
   The Observer, Aug. 12, 1984, p. 30.

3 What on earth has this synchronised swimming got to do with anything, let alone sport?
Frank Keating

The Guardian, Aug. 8, 1984.

4 Synchronized swimming is a skilful art.
George Rackham

Synchronized Swimming, 1968, p. 21.

5 Sculling is the bread and butter of synchro.
George Rackham

Ibid., p. 194.

6 Synchronized swimmers may look like cupcakes, but they're tough cookies.
Demmie Stathoplos

Sports Illustrated, Aug. 2, 1982, p. 28.

TABLE TENNIS

1 The 'obvious' maxim which isn't obvious is; SPEED (of hit) doesn't earn so many points as CHANGE OF SPEED (of hit).
Jack Carrington

Modern Table Tennis (1938), 1966, p. 81.

2 Style is the outward pattern of play, not to be confused with technique, which is the inside working of the feet-hands-eyes-brain-bat-ball complex.
Jack Carrington

Progressive Table Tennis, 1970, p. 17.

3 The secret of table tennis is the secret of all ball games; ball control.
Ken Stanley

Table Tennis – A New Approach, 1959, p. 13.

4 In no other sport is there so broad and universal an appeal
   which, in its higher phases, combines the psychology of bridge,
   the grace of eurhythmics, the footwork of dancing, the lightning
   cut-and-thrust of fencing, the waywardness of golf, the ball
   cunning of billiards and the agility of athletics.
   Leslie Woollard

   Table Tennis, 1952, p. 7.

5 Individualism provides the zest, life and colour of a sport and
   there is no game more individualistic than Table Tennis.
   Leslie Woollard

   Ibid., p. 21.

TENPIN BOWLING

1 Whether you bowl as an individual or as a member of a team,
   the challenge of making a better score is always there.
   Anthony A. Annarino
   Bowling: Individualized Instructional Program, 1973, p. 2.

2 Too many times a pro bowler is classed with the average fun
   bowler. That's like equating a touch football game with the
   Super Bowl.
   Dick Ritger

   The New York Times, Apr. 17, 1979.

3 The pins become an object of frustration, not just to be knocked
   down, but to be conquered.
   Don Russell
   (On the attitude of some league bowlers)

   Bowling Now, 1980, p. 138.

TOBOGGANING

1 There is one Mecca, there is one St Peter's, there is one Cresta. As is Mecca to the Mohammedan, as is St Peter's to the Catholic, so is the Cresta Run at St Moritz to the tobogganer.
E. B. Benson
Quoted by Michael Seth-Smith.

The Cresta Run, 1976, p. 6.

2 (The flexible sled) . . . the beginning of the triumph of lugeing.
The Oxford Companion to Sports and Games, 1975, p. 1035.

UNDERWATER SWIMMING

1 One man using a hand spear, and his physical prowess to hunt in the depths may possibly still be termed a sportsman. But divers armed with powered spear guns who wear air cylinders on their backs deserve only the adjective butcher . . .
David Hodgson
Dive! Dive! Dive!: A Sport Diver's Guide, 1975, p. 2.

2 Diving, as we do it for sport, is not dangerous if approached in a sensible manner. By sensible I mean with a 'touch of cowardice'.
John Reseck Jr.
Scuba, Safe and Simple, 1975, p. 11.

3 In diving, there is one law of nature that seems to dominate. That law is pressure.
John Reseck Jr.

Ibid., p. 78.

4 Medical problems for the diver are like accident problems for the motorist.
John Reseck Jr.

Ibid., p. 88.

5 The thermocline is a weird sort of thing.
Fred M. Roberts
Basic Scuba: Self-Contained Underwater Breathing Apparatus,
1963, p. 19.

6 The modern diving lung is more than just another piece of diving equipment. It is your life!
Fred M. Roberts

Ibid., p. 48.

7 A diver must be able to understand sufficient physiology to realise the limitations of his own physique; enough physics to appreciate the effects of a hyperbaric environment, and be sufficiently practical to understand the workings of his equipment.
The British Sub Aqua Club Diving Manual, 1978, p. 9.

VIOLENCE

1 Sport legitimises violence, thereby laundering it acceptably clean . . . the mugger in the parking lot is a villain; the mugger on the playing field is a hero.
Don Atyeo
Quoted by Simon Inglis.
The Guardian, Oct. 5, 1985, p. 13.

2 Sports used to be appropriately rugged . . .
Teri Engler
(On the increase in sports violence)
'Kill 'Em! Sports Violence and the Law', *Update,* Spring., 1983.

3 Violence surrounds and permeates modern sports to such a degree that it is not unreasonable to suggest that there is a necessary connection between them.
Jeffrey H. Goldstein
'Sports Violence', *National Forum:*
The Phi Kappa Phi Journal, vol. 62, no. 1, Winter, 1982, p. 9.

4 It is not competition per se that increases aggression, among either players or fans, but the nature and spirit of that competition.
Jeffrey H. Goldstein
Ibid., p. 11.

5 Violent outbursts are news and good behaviour is not.
Denis Howell
Speech at a conference for Sports Ministers of the Council of Europe, *British Journal of Physical Education*, vol. 8, no. 6, Nov., 1977, p. 175.

6 Consistent and uncompromising opposition to violence in sport will yield results only if we know its underpinnings. There seem to be two principal . . . constantly growing incidence of crime in the capitalist countries and the increasing commercial-isation of sport.
Roman Kiselev
Sport in the USSR, Jul., 1983, p. 33.

7 Serious sport has nothing to do with fair play. It is bound up with hatred, jealousy, boastfulness, disregard of all rules and sadistic pleasure in witnessing violence: in other words it is war minus the shooting.
George Orwell
Quoted in *Inside Track, The Sunday Times*, Jan. 8, 1984.

8 Inter-personal and property vandalism in and around professional football grounds is currently running a close second to political deviance in Grosvenor Square in the 'Top Twenty' of Society's social problems.
Ian Taylor
'Football Mad: A Speculative Sociology of Football Hooliganism',
in Eric Dunning (ed.), *The Sociology of Sport:*
A Selection of Readings, 1971, p. 352.

VOLLEYBALL

1 From all my years of involvement in volleyball, I am convinced of one thing: Coaches cannot invent new ways of passing or setting the ball. They can only refine skills and techniques – change little things – to develop better progressions or methods of instruction.
Russ Rose
Scholastic Coach, Nov., 1981, p. 50.

2 That women's volleyball is a vociferous sport is also one of its peculiar charms.
Stanislav Tokarev
Sport in the USSR, Oct., 1983, p. 17.

3 Volleyball is a dandy game and more besides.
Peter Wardale
Volleyball: Skills and Tactics, 1964, p. 15.

4 No player likes to think of himself as a puppet with the coach in the background manipulating the strings.
Peter Wardale
Ibid., p. 55.

WEIGHTLIFTING

1 The one sport which will lay the foundation of success in all others – the one alone which can ensure pre-eminence in all others.
John Murray
(On Weightlifting)
Introduction to W. A. Pullum, *Weight-Lifting Made Easy and Interesting*.

2 For me this man has always been not only the personification of
   strength, but that of inspired strength, of lofty human qualities.
   Yuri Vlasov
   (On Paul Anderson)
                                        Sport in the USSR, Jun., 1979, p. 17.

3 The jerk was and remains, without doubt, the main record in
   weightlifting.
   Yuri Vlasov
                                                                    Ibid.

WINNING

1 To the religiously devout, God is everything; to the American
   athlete, it would seem, Winning is everything.
   Arnold Beisser
                                    The Madness in Sport, 1977, p. 145.

2 In pro football, it's obvious that you must win. In college football there's sometimes talk of other goals, but when you get
   right down to it that's what really matters there, too.
   John Bridgers
                        'Scorecard', *Sports Illustrated*, Jan. 6, 1969, p. 8.

3 Australia's National Sport – Winning.
   John A. Daley
                                Title of Article in William Johnson (ed.),
                                    Sport and Physical Education, 1980.

4 Whatever the cynics may have to say, the manner of winning
   is important . . .
   Geoff Dyson
                        Athletics Weekly, vol. 26, no. 41, Oct. 7, 1972, p. 21.

5 Will-to-win is not the key to Australia's success in sport, but it
is an essential part of the compound of responsible factors.
H. Gordon
'The Reasons Why', in T. D. Jaques and G. R. Pavia (ed.),
Sport in Australia: Selected Readings in
Physical Activity, 1973, p. 96.

6 Success is important but defeats are valuable.
C. M. Jones
Bowls: How to Become a Champion, 1972, p. 137.

7 Everyone has a will to win but very few have a will to prepare
to win.
Vince Lombardi.
Quoted by Dr Robert D. Steadward.
AJHPER, The Australian Journal For Health,
Physical Education and Recreation, Autumn, no. 91, 1981.

8 Winning isn't everything; it's the only thing.
Vince Lombardi
(Attributed)

9 The desire to win is sometimes so strong that sport cannot
contain it; when this natural desire is reinforced with political
pressures it is small wonder that on occasions the structure of
the sporting event bursts asunder
P. C. McIntosh
Sport in Society, 1963, p. 199.

10 The win ethic is epitomized in professional sport where, irres-
pective of the attitudes of the players, the sole function in terms
of the organization and consumers is to win.
Alan Metcalfe
British Journal of Physical Education,
vol. 6, no. 1, Jan–Feb., 1975, p. 8.

11 Winning is both excellence and vindication in the face of the
gods.
Michael Novak
The New York Times, Jan. 30, 1977.

12 When you win you eat better, sleep better and your beer tastes
better. And your wife looks like Gina Lollobrigida.
Johnny Pesky
'Scorecard', *Sports Illustrated*, May 20, 1963.

13 Everything about being a professional sportsman is about winning.
Graeme Souness

> Quoted by *The Guardian*, Jan. 20, 1984.

14 Americans are experts at winning, but still amateurs at losing.
Edward R. Walsh

> *The New York Times*, Mar. 20, 1977.

15 Because the dread of losing dominates our sporting lives, we have bleached the fun out of colorful games.
Edward R. Walsh

> Ibid.

16 There's more to victory than final scores and banner headlines. Let's emphasize the fringe benefits of competition, winning friends, trust, respect, confidence, knowledge, skill, happiness and fun.
Edward R. Walsh

> Ibid.

17 Everything a champion does must be in terms of winning.
Les Woodland

> *Cycle Racing: Training to Win*, 1975, p. 134.

WOMEN

1 Riding as an exercise for women below forty-five years of age is to be condemned. Of the young married women who ride to hounds about sixty per cent are childless; and of the remainder few have more than one child. No girl over thirteen years of age should be allowed to ride much if at all, and then only at an amble. The reasons are obvious, but cannot be given in detail here.
James Cantlie

> *Physical Efficiency*, 1906, p. 189.

2 Sport was the first great separator of the sexes.
Robert Lipsyte
National Forum: The Phi Kappa Phi Journal, vol. 62, no. 1,
1982, p. 29.

3 'Women in Sport' is no longer an issue. It is a fact.
Suzi Olcott
Scholastic Coach, Aug., 1979, p. 61.

4 Frequently track and field events are relegated to the realm of
sweat and muscles, unsuitable for the 'gentler sex'. There is
nothing wrong with sweat, and a strong woman whose figure
stands up for itself is much to be admired.
John T. Powell
'How to Teach the High Jump to Girls',
Proceedings, First National Institute on Girls' Sports,
1963, Norman, USA, p. 119.

5 Physical activity should never be a threat to femininity but
should be part of the development of it.
Paul D. Robinson
(Attributed)

6 The female of our species has been hindered by the propagation
of myths regarding her abilities to withstand stress, to perform
heavy work, to run, jump or just plain play.
C. L. Wells
'The Female Athlete: Myths and Superstitions
Put to Rest', in E. J. Burke (ed.),
Towards an Understanding of Human Performance, 1978,
p. 39.

WRESTLING

1 The best offense in wrestling is often good defense.
Dariel Daniel
Scholastic Coach, Nov., 1980, p. 44.

2 No one has a corner on fundamentals and holds in wrestling.
   Joe Gilas
   'A Complete Wrestling Program', The Coaching Clinic (ed.),
   Best of Wrestling from The Coaching Clinic, p. 22.

3 The three main avenues that lead to consistently strong wrestling programs are good athletes, good coaches, and good
   competition (that brings out the best in the first two).
   Joseph M. Puggelli
   Scholastic Coach, Oct., 1980, p. 46.

4 Freestyle and Greco-Roman wrestling are in complete philo-
   sophic and general technical agreement.
   Joseph M. Puggelli
   Scholastic Coach, Dec., 1980, p. 27.

5 With the possible exception of the knockout in boxing, nothing
   can match the Freestyle Throw for dramatic effect upon the
   outcome of a contest.
   Joseph Puggelli
   Scholastic Coach, Mar., 1981, p. 88.

6 Like an Olympian wrestling:
   William Shakespeare
   (Nestor), *Troilus and Cressida*, act IV, sc. V, l. 193.

7 To give a Cornish hug is a proverbial expression.
   Joseph Strutt
   The Sports and Pastimes of the People of England,
   1830, book II, ch. 11, p. 80.

YACHTING

1 There is never a 'right' time to sail across the Atlantic alone.
   There is only 'now' or 'never'.
   David Blagden
   Very Willing Griffin, 1973, intro.

2 Racing may begin earlier than the gun, but the start is when the cards come down.
John Chamier

> *Small Boat and Dinghy Sailing*, 1963, p. 84.

3 A yacht race, it may be said, is not merely a contest of speed but also a battle of wits.
Francis B. Cooke

> *The Care of Small Craft*, p. 6.

4 Good seamanship brings out the finest human qualities – courage, resourcefulness, vigilance and endurance.
H.R.H. The Duke of Edinburgh

> Preface to E. H. Haylock, *Water Wisdom*, 1966.

5 The three equal contributory factors in a successful racing boat are the helmsman, the crew and the boat.
Bob Fisher

> *Crewing Racing Dinghies and Keelboats*, 1976, p. 12.

6 Except for the hedonist, the pleasure derived from any leisure activity is directly proportional to the effort put in. This is even more true in competitive sport.
Bob Fisher

> *Ibid.*, p. 17.

7 Like it or not, small boat racing is now an athletic sport.
Bob Fisher

> *Ibid.*, p. 25.

8 Seamanship still wins races.
Bob Fisher

> *Ibid.*, p. 156.

9 In the field of action, sailing offers greater thrills than many sports, with less risk than most, for it provides a sensation of great speed without the necessity for travelling very fast.
John Fisher

> *The New Small Boat Sailing*, 1953, p. 14.

10 One who in a crisis forgets nautical language and shouts, 'For God's sake turn left'.
Michael Green
(Definition of a Coarse Sailor)

> *The Art of Coarse Sailing*, 1962, p. 7.

11   There are few things in the world so fascinating, so rewarding, or so productive of the good in man as the art of sailing.
Peter Heaton
Sailing (1949), 1978, p. 15.

12   Of all things made by man there is nothing so lovely as a sailing boat.
Peter Heaton
Ibid., p. 16.

13   There is one good rule in helmsmanship – let the boat do the sailing.
Peter Heaton
Ibid., p. 152.

14   Winning is all-important. Anything less is second class, but it is of paramount importance that racing should be enjoyed.
Peter Hunter
'The Psychology and Philosophy of Crewing',
in Bob Fisher, *Crewing Racing Dinghies and Keelboats*,
1976, p. 30.

15   Good seamanship is eight parts common sense.
Jack Knights
Sailing: Step by Step, 1961, p. 12.

16   Sailing is full of unstraightforward names for quite straightforward things.
Jack Knights
Ibid., p. 25.

17   Sailing can satisfy nearly all the senses and stir all the emotions.
W. N. D. Lang
The Art and Sport of Sailing, 1968, p. 9.

18   The theory and the practice of sailing are undoubtedly uneasy bedfellows.
C. A. Marchaj
Sailing Theory and Practice, 1964, preface.

19   The coverage of the America's Cup is unbelievable. Never have the media done so much for so little.
Herman L. Masin
Scholastic Coach, Nov., 1980, p. 18.

20 There is a veritable psychosis among racing men over the sail
'which pulls'.
Yves-Louis Pinaud
Sailing from Start to Finish, translated by
James and Ingeborg Moore, 1971, p. 188.

21 As when a bride is brought into a community of established
housewives, all eyes will be turned to see how the new ship
behaves.
D. A. Rayner
Safety in Small Craft, 1961, p. 21.

22 A ship, even the most humble, that spreads the silent planes
of her sails to the power of the wind, is a very perfect machine.
D. A. Rayner
Ibid., p. 39.

23 The endless contest with the sea is the finer for being obscure;
for being fought without the plaudits of spectators.
D. A. Rayner
Ibid., p. 60.

24 The handling of a ship, no matter how large or how small, is
but the expression of her master's quality, and beyond that
limit no man may go without meeting fear and disaster.
D. A. Rayner
Ibid.

25 The highest reward of all sports, even competitive ones, is the
conscious savouring of perfect performance.
J. Russell
Yachtmaster Offshore: The Art of Seamanship, 1977, p. 7.

26 The triumph of being first past the finishing post is transient,
the faultlessly timed and co-ordinated output of the last ounce
of energy into the sport that took you there is imperishable.
J. Russell
Ibid., p. 7.

27 Ropes are a ship's sinews.
J. Russell
Ibid., p. 22.

28 But ships are but boards, sailors but men:
    William Shakespeare
            (Shylock), *The Merchant of Venice*, act I, sc. III, l. 22.

29 The things that drive a man to ocean sailing must be pretty
    much the same as those that drive him to drink. For of all
    sports, this is the most habit forming, the most expensive, the
    most exasperating, the most soothing, the most strenuous, the
    most uncomfortable and the most fun.
    Hugh Whall
                        Sports Illustrated, Jul. 4, 1966, p. 33.

SUBJECT INDEX

For a note on the arrangement of this index see page x.

Honest: h. angler, Angling 28
Hooliganism: philosophy of h.,
  Spectators 4
Horse: polo mount . . . is a h., Polo
  3; A h. is a vain thing, Religion
  11
Humiliated: In no sport . . . can
  you be more h., Boxing 58
Humility: carried modesty to the
  length of h., Cricket 4
Hungry: athletes must be . . . h.,
  Drama 2
Hunt: played golf . . . so I could
  afford to h., Golf 20
Hunted: the angler is the h.,
  Angling 25
Hunter: The fish is the h., Angling
  25
Hypocrisy: H. . . . . culprit where
  amateurism is concerned,
  Amateurism 5; old-fashioned
  American h., Football
  (American) 6

Ignobility: arenas into cockpits of
  i., Spectators 3
Imperialism: world sport
  parallels . . . i., Politics 2
Improvisation: I. is the hardest skill
  of all to counter, Football
  (Association) 14
Indecisiveness: i. . . . . damaging to
  performance, Athletes 7
Independence: great charms of
  archery is its i., Archery 3; it
  fosters the spirit of i., Modern
  Pentathlon 1
India: On the plains of I. . . . .
  cricket finds a home, Cricket 32
Indifference: Racing . . . produces
  no i., Horse Racing 4
Individualism: I. provides the zest,
  life and colour of a sport, Table
  Tennis 5
Individuality: every game its own
  i., Cricket 48
Initiative: effective use of i., Life
  Saving 3
Instincts: All fielders must have

good i., Baseball 16;
satisfies . . . i. of men, Climbing
39; Squash . . . appeals to our
basic i., Squash Rackets 6
Intellectual: equal to an i. throwing
  a good punch, Boxing 56; moral
  and i. balance, Climbing 14
Intellectuals: disdain many i. feel
  for the activities of the masses,
  Football (Australian Rules) 6;
  They are not all i., Rugby
  League 4
Ireland: coast of I., Climbing 54

Javelin: I once threw the j.,
  Athletics 16; hurling a j.,
  Philosophy 7
Jockeys: no more ethical than j.,
  Cricket 26
Jogging: J. is . . . natural, Fitness
  18; squash . . . less boring than
  j., Squash Rackets 5
Judge: j. and the referee, Boxing
  41
Judgement: result . . . without
  recourse to j., Sport 20
Justice: J. does not always triumph,
  Sportsmanship 13

Kicking: K. across goals, Football
  (Australian Rules) 2
Kill: without the hunt and the k.,
  Field Sports 11
Knowledge: scientific k., Caving 3

Labour: Peace be at your l. honest
  fisherman, Angling 19
Last: Nice guys finish l.,
  Sportsmanship 6
Laughter: death to it – l.,
  Spectators 6
Law: like a poor man's right in the
  l., Angling 21; such is the l.,
  Climbing 29; The advantage l.,
  Rugby Union 41; That l. is
  pressure, Underwater
  Swimming 3

AUTHOR INDEX

For a note on the arrangement of this index see page x.